DEC Recommended Practices

A Comprehensive Guide For Practical Application in Early Intervention/Early Childhood Special Education

(second printing)

Bridging the gap between research and practice, the book *DEC Recommended Practices* provides guidance on effective practices for working with young children with disabilities. The recommended practices are based on a review and synthesis of the research literature and the practices identified as critical by various stakeholders in early intervention/early childhood special education.

The book contains recommended practices in the following areas:

- Assessment—*John Neisworth and Stephen Bagnato*
- Child-focused interventions—*Mark Wolery*
- Family-based practices—*Carol Trivette and Carl Dunst*
- Interdisciplinary models—*R.A. McWilliam*
- Technology applications—*Kathleen Stremel*
- Policies, procedures, and systems change—*Gloria Harbin and Christine Salisbury*
- Personnel preparation—*Patricia Miller and Vicki Stayton*

The second printing of *DEC Recommended Practices* is easier to use than ever and has been completely updated with additional resources and advice, program checklists for both parents and administrators, and two new chapters dealing with the real-life experiences of users. Put *DEC Recommended Practices* to work for your students today!

Visit our website to view companion pieces to this text, read about other exciting and useful products or to place an order. Click on the 'Store' tab.

Division for Early Childhood (DEC)
www.dec-sped.org

y^{O}u^{n}g
Exceptio$_{n}$al
children

The *Young Exceptional Children (YEC)* Monograph Series is designed for teachers, early care and education personnel, administrators, therapists, family members, and others who work with or on behalf of children, ages birth to eight, who have identified disabilities, developmental delays, are gifted/talented, or are at risk of future developmental delays or school difficulties.

This series offers great ideas on some of the most important topics in early intervention and early childhood special education. Each Monograph is focused on a single topic and includes a carefully selected collection of articles to translate research findings into effective and use-ful strategies for practitioners and families.

**Monograph Series 1 – Practical Ideas
for Addressing Challenging Behavior**

Monograph Series 2 – Natural Environments and Inclusion

Monograph Series 3 – Teaching Strategies

**Monograph Series 4 – Assessment: Gathering
Meaningful Information**

Monograph Series 5 – Family-Based Practices

Monograph Series 6 – Interdisciplinary Teams

**Monograph Series 7 – Supporting Early Literacy
Development in Young Children**

Monograph Series 8 – Social Emotional Development

**Monograph Series 9 – Linking Curriculum
to Child and Family Outcomes**

**Monograph Series 10 – Early Intervention for Infants and
Toddlers and Their Families: Practices and Outcomes**

Visit our website to read more about this series, view other exciting and useful products or to place an order. Click on the 'Store' tab.

Division for Early Childhood (DEC)
www.dec-sped.org

young Exceptional children

Monograph Series No. 2

Natural Environments and Inclusion

THE DIVISION FOR EARLY CHILDHOOD
OF THE COUNCIL FOR EXCEPTIONAL CHILDREN

Susan Sandall and Michaelene Ostrosky
Co-Editors

Disclaimer

The opinions and information contained in the articles in this publication are those of the authors of the respective articles and not necessarily those of the co-editors of *Young Exceptional Children (YEC) Monograph Series* or of the Division for Early Childhood. Accordingly, the Division for Early Childhood assumes no liability or risk that may be incurred as a consequence, directly or indirectly, of the use and application of any of the contents of this publication.

The DEC does not perform due diligence on advertisers, exhibitors, or their products or services, and cannot endorse or guarantee that their offerings are suitable or accurate.

ISSN 1096-2506 • ISBN 978-0-9819-327-1-2

Printed in the United States of America

Published and Distributed by:

Division for Early Childhood (DEC)
27 Fort Missoula Road, Ste. 2
Missoula, MT 59804
(406) 543-0872 • FAX (406) 543-0887
Email: dec@dec-sped.org
www.dec-sped.org

features

A Message from the Editors

Welcome to the second issue of the Young Exceptional Children Monograph Series. In this issue we address the topic of Natural Environments and Inclusion. The topic was selected based on the results of a survey of DEC members and conference attendees.

A monograph focusing on natural environments and inclusion is timely. More and more children with disabilities and other special needs are participating in settings and activities with children without disabilities. The providers in these settings seek assistance in assuring quality care and education for all children. DEC's position statement on inclusion clearly spells out our organization's beliefs about inclusive practices. You are encouraged to copy this statement and share it with your colleagues.

Why do we use two terms to refer to the process of including children with disabilities in home and community settings? Inclusion is a viable service option for preschool children with disabilities. Over 50% of all preschool children with disabilities who are receiving educational services are in some form of inclusive setting (U.S. Department of Education, 1998). We believe that many additional children participate in other recreation, child care, or religious activities with their typically developing peers. Despite the strong research base on preschool inclusion and access to inclusive programs and services, a number of issues and concerns remain. Odom (2000) reported that many of these issues have to do with the quality of services, the intensity and specificity of services, creation of meaningful social experiences for children, and a variety of issues related to the infrastructure needed to ensure effective and sustainable inclusive services for children. Some of these important issues are addressed in this monograph.

The term natural environments appears in Part C of IDEA. Natural environments are "settings that are natural or normal for the child's age peers who have no disabilities" (34 CFR Part 303.18). While the term has appeared in the law since 1989, the 1997 reauthorization strengthened the requirement. Many states, local programs, and early interventionists find themselves in the midst of change. They may be struggling with a variety of issues related to providing comprehensive, coordinated, family-centered services for infants and toddlers with disabilities and their families in natural settings. Articles in this monograph address the questions of the "when" and "where" of early intervention in natural settings; articles also address the question of "how" early intervention is provided.

Two articles tackle the many questions that providers and families may have about changes in early intervention. Walsh, Rous, and Lutzer use examples from states as well as excerpts from the law and regulations to provide clarification. McWilliam writes about the potential benefits of these changes. He provides practical directions for families and the professionals who work on their behalf. Child care centers are natural environments for many children. Craig, Haggart, Gold, and Hull point out that the child care director is the key to successful inclusive child care. Drawing from their experiences in the child care arena, they share their findings and practical strategies for working with child care directors. In their article, Dunst, Herter, and Shields help us think about how to take full advantage of natural learning opportunities in a wide variety of community-based activities and settings. The reader will find specific ways to identify young children's interests in order to enhance their participation in the community.

Three articles focus on preschool children. Horn and Sandall address the itinerant teaching model, providing readers with strategies for effectively implementing this model. Diamond and Stacey remind us to think about all of the children who participate in inclusive classrooms and settings. They use their experience in inclusive preschools to provide the reader with useful advice to ensure that preschool is a valuable experience that nurtures positive attitudes. Hull, Venn, Lee, and Van Buren discuss the importance of planning for and supporting preschoolers as they participate in a variety of activities and settings. Finally, in Catlett's column, *Resources Within Reason*, you will find additional resources related to the topic of natural environments and inclusion.

Taken together, these articles focus our attention on important issues. The authors provide us with suggestions and strategies to help open the doors for children and their families to successfully participate in natural settings. We express our appreciation to the authors and to the reviewers who provided thoughtful and careful consideration of all of the manuscripts submitted for the second *YEC* monograph.

References

Odom, S.L. (2000). Preschool inclusion: What we know and where we go from here. *Topics in Early Childhood Special Education, 20*(1), 20-27.

U.S. Department of Education (1998). *To assure the free appropriate public education of all children with disabilities: Twentieth annual report to Congress on the implementation of the Individuals with Disabilities Act.* Washington, DC: Author.

Co-Editors: Susan Sandall
(206) 543-4011
ssandall@u.washington.edu

Michaelene Ostrosky
(217) 333-0260
ostrosky@uiuc.edu

THE DIVISION FOR EARLY CHILDHOOD

Division for Early Childhood
of the Council for Exceptional Children
Position on Inclusion

Adopted: April, 1993
Revised December, 1993
Reaffirmed, 1996
Updated, 2000

Inclusion, as a value, supports the right of all children, regardless of abilities, to participate actively in natural settings within their communities. Natural settings are those in which the child would spend time had he or she not had a disability. These settings include, but are not limited to home, preschool, nursery schools, Head Start programs, kindergartens, neighborhood school classrooms, child care, places of worship, recreational (such as community playgrounds and community events) and other settings that all children and families enjoy.

DEC supports and advocates that young children and their families have full and successful access to health, social, educational, and other support services that promote full participation in family and community life. DEC values the cultural, economic, and educational diversity of families and supports a family-guided process for identifying a program of service. As young children participate in group settings (such as preschool, play groups, child care, kindergarten) their active participation should be guided by developmentally and individually appropriate curriculum. Access to and participation in the age appropriate general curriculum becomes central to the identification and provision of specialized support services.

To implement inclusive practices DEC supports: (1) the continued development, implementation, evaluation, and dissemination of full inclusion supports, services, and systems that are of high quality for all children; (2) the development of preservice and inservice training programs that prepare families, service providers, and administrators to develop and work within inclusive settings; (3) collaboration among key stakeholders to implement flexible fiscal and administrative procedures in support of inclusion; (4) research that contributes to our knowledge of recommended practice; and (5) the restructuring and unification of social, educational, health, and intervention supports and services to make them more responsive to the needs of all children and families. Ultimately the implementation of inclusive practice must lead to optimal developmental benefit for each individual child and family.

Endorsed by NAEYC - April 1994, April 1998

Permission to copy not required—distribution encouraged.

The Federal IDEA Natural Environments Provisions

Making it Work

Sharon Walsh, M.A., Walsh Taylor, Inc.
Beth Rous, M.Ed., University of Kentucky
Christie Lutzer, M.A., University of Kentucky

The implementation of the natural environments mandates within the Individuals with Disabilities Education Act (IDEA) have provided a number of opportunities, as well as challenges to state and local Part C systems across the country. In designing successful statewide natural environment implementation plans, state lead agencies must address a number of issues including how natural environments are defined, what settings are appropriate, the parent's role in these decisions, and transition. The purpose of this article is to describe the federal requirements and provide examples of how the federal government and states are providing guidance to address the natural environments requirements. Information on state implementation was obtained through a review of available state Part C documents.

The IDEA, Part C natural environments requirements are consistent with generally accepted principles of early childhood practice. It has long been recognized that the provision of early intervention services should take place in natural environments (Erwin, 1996; Noonan & McCormick, 1993), those in which the family routinely interacts since the family serves as the primary means of support in the early years of a child's life (Erwin & Schreiber, 1999). Thurman (1997) defines early intervention within the context of "an array of services that is put in place through a partnership with families" (p. 3). These services include promoting the development of the child within the framework of the family, and ensuring that the family has the information and skills they consider necessary to participate actively in supporting their child's development. Bronfenbrenner (1979) proposed direct links between a child's social and cognitive development and environments in which he/she spends time. Therefore, the developmental process must take into consideration the complex interactions between the child and the microsystems within which he/she exists, those environments most immediate to the child such as the family, child care programs, and community centers.

National organizations such as the Division for Early Childhood (DEC) of The Council for Exceptional Children (CEC) and the National Association for the Education of Young Children (NAEYC) have developed statements supporting the use of natural environments in early childhood as part of developmentally appropriate practices (Bredekamp & Copple, 1997; DEC, 1994). The IDEA Infant and Toddler Coordinators Association (IDEA/ITCA), representing the state Part C Systems, approved a position paper in April 2000, which states "the Association fully supports the provision of early intervention services within the context of families' activities and routines in meeting the natural environments requirements under Part C of IDEA" (p. 2). They further state that "providing services in natural environments is not just the law, but more importantly, it reflects the core mission of early intervention, which is to support families to provide learning opportunities for their child within the activities, routines, and events of everyday life" (p. 1).

In response to the field's understanding of the importance of providing services to very young children within natural settings, the Part C regulations have, since 1989, required that, to the extent appropriate for a child, early intervention services take place in settings in which children without disabilities participate. The 1997 reauthorization of the Individuals with Disabilities Education Act (IDEA) strengthened the requirement that early intervention services be provided to infants and toddlers (birth to age 3) with disabilities in natural environments, to the extent appropriate to the child.

The IDEA, Part C statute and regulations define natural environments as "settings that are natural or normal for the child's age peers who have no disabilities" (34 CFR Part 303.18). Such environments may include the child's home, child care setting, or a neighborhood play group. One benefit of providing services in such settings is the early interventionist can model effective techniques for the parent or child care provider. These interventions can then be used throughout the child's daily routines, at times when the young child is physiologically and psychologically ready for interaction (Kleinhammer-Tramill & Rosenkoetter, 1994).

IDEA '97 requires all states participating in Part C to develop statewide systems to address the needs of infants and toddlers receiving early intervention services. Since all states have opted to participate in Part C, each must develop and implement policies and procedures to ensure that "to the maximum extent appropriate, early intervention services are provided in natural environments, and the provision of early intervention services for any infant or toddler occurs in a setting other than a natural environment only if early intervention cannot be achieved satisfactorily for the infant or toddler in a natural environment" (34 CFR Part 303.167(c)).

The decisions about where services are to be provided are made within the Individualized Family Service Plan (IFSP) process by the IFSP team, which includes the child's parents. The IFSP for each infant or toddler receiving early intervention services and their family must include a "statement of the natural environments...in which early intervention services will be provided, and a justification of the extent, if any, to which the services will not be provided in a natural environment" (34 CFR Part 303.344(d)(1)(ii)).

While federal requirements and effective practice principles provide a compelling framework for the provision of early intervention services within natural environments, there still exists considerable disagreement and confusion about its implementation. Furthermore, even though many parents and providers enthusiastically endorse full implementation of these requirements, successful implementation remains a challenge. In designing successful statewide natural environment implementation plans, state lead agencies are addressing a number of these issues and challenges, several of which are discussed below.

It's Not Only About Place

The use of natural environments for infants and toddlers is based on the premise that child and family needs can be met in environments that are natural for the family. However, implementation of natural environments goes beyond "place." As the child and family outcomes, as well as family resources, priorities, and concerns change, the environments in which services are provided may also change. In fact, the environments in which services are provided may be continually changing throughout the family's involvement in the Part C system.

Several states have provided direction on the issue of "place" within the natural environments mandate. For example, the Texas Part C system provided much of the earliest guidance about how to successfully implement natural environments requirements. This includes incorporation of the concepts of natural environments throughout the entire IFSP process beginning at referral and continuing through transition.

The Colorado Part C system, called Early Childhood Connections, states its belief and policy in "A Guidebook: Early Intervention Supports and Services in Everyday Routines, Activities, and Places in Colorado" (December, 1999) as follows: "Supports and services are most effective when they are provided in families' everyday routines, activities, and places. *Where* and *when* supports and services are provided are essential elements of quality. Equally important are the elements of *what* and *how* services are delivered. Services provided in everyday routines, activities, and places must also be developmentally appropriate and relevant to families' lives" (p. i).

In March 2000, the Indiana First Steps Part C system issued a directive, stating among other things:

... the process of identifying the natural environment is to begin with a discussion with the family that identifies the daily routines and activities of their child and their family, including the family's schedule and other activities and demands. The discussion must identify the activities within the child's or the family's routine that are important and need to be enhanced in order for their child to be successful. The team, including the parent, is to discuss and select those activities that will most appropriately support the outcomes identified in the child's Individualized Family Services Plan (IFSP). (p. 2)

What Settings are Natural Settings?

If natural environments are more than "place," then one challenge is how to define those settings that are considered natural to families. The premise behind the natural environments movement is very similar to that of least restrictive environments for children under Part B of IDEA: to the extent appropriate to their needs, children with disabilities must be educated with their typically developing peers. The similarities are especially true for preschoolers with disabilities. According to the U.S. Secretary of Education in the "Analysis of Comments and Changes" in the March 12, 1999, publication of the Part B regulations at 34 CFR Part 300, "The full continuum of alternative placements at 34 CFR 300.551, including integrated placement options, such as community-based settings with typically developing age peers, must be available to preschool children with disabilities" (p.12639).

However, for Part C, natural environments take into consideration the need to develop the capacity of the family to meet their child's individual needs, all within the context of the family's own needs and priorities. The IDEA/ITCA (2000) defines natural groups as:

... groups that would continue to exist with or without children with disabilities. Groups that are not 'natural groups' include only children with disabilities. However, even the most 'natural' of groups is not a natural setting for a particular child if it is not part of that child's family's routine or community. (p. 2)

The Missouri First Steps Part C System issued a Technical Assistance Bulletin in January, 1999 indicating that for agencies to meet the test of providing services in natural environments, each would have to be "considered community settings in which children without disabilities participate" (p. 3). The Missouri Departments of Health, Mental Health, and Education have set the goal that by the year 2001, the substantial majority of children receiving services in First Steps will be receiving them in natural environments where the majority of children do not have disabilities.

One of the more controversial questions is about services provided in clinic or office settings. According to the IDEA/ITCA (2000), "service settings that are not 'natural settings' include clinics, hospitals, therapists' offices, rehabilitation centers, and segregated group settings. This includes any setting designed to serve children based on categories of disabilities or selected for the convenience of service providers" (p. 2). However, there are times when these settings may be appropriate and justified based on child circumstances (e.g., while a child is staying in a hospital for treatment).

Clarification of the Justification

Federal regulations provide for "a justification of the extent, if any, to which the services will not be provided in a natural environment" (34 CFR 303.344(d)(1)(ii)). Many states provide guidance for the establishment of a rationale for services outside the natural environment. In some cases states are additionally providing information on the prohibition of using Part C funds or state funds to provide services that are in settings that do not meet these requirements.

The Office of Special Education Programs (OSEP) at the U.S. Department of Education (M. Elder, personal communication, July 17, 1998) clarified the use of Part C funds as follows:

... if the parents do not consent to a particular location for a service specified in the IFSP, the State may not use Part C funds to provide that service in a location different from that identified on the IFSP. The parents are free to reject any service(s) on the IFSP by not providing written consent for that service(s) or by withdrawing consent after first providing it. If the parents do not provide consent for a particular early intervention service, which also includes the location, that service may not be provided. .... All funds used to implement the early intervention system under Part C must be used consistent with Part C. Thus, the State cannot circumvent the requirement to provide early intervention services in natural environments by using State funds that are budgeted for early intervention services under Part C and used to satisfy the nonsupplanting requirement.

Connecticut's Birth to Three System (1999) has been working on implementing natural environments for a number of years and has provided much of the guidance other states are adopting. The state's April, 1999 Revised *Service Guidelines 2 Natural Environments: Intervention Guidance for Service Providers and Families* states that in completing justification on an IFSP, the IFSP team must:

1. Explain how and why the IFSP team determined that the child's outcome(s) could not be met if the service were provided in the child's natural environment with supplementary supports provided by the Birth to Three program. If the child has not made satisfactory progress toward an outcome in a natural environment, the explanation must include a description of why alternative natural environments have not been selected or why it is inappropriate to modify the outcome;

2. Explain how services provided in this location will be generalized to support the child's ability to function in his/her natural environment; and

3. Develop a plan, with timelines and supports necessary, to allow the child's outcomes to be satisfactorily achieved in his/her natural environments. (p.11)

Parent Choice

Family involvement is the cornerstone of Part C program design. DEC (1993) defines family participation by stating that families "[are] equal members in, can join together with staff and can take part in all aspects of the early intervention system, including all aspects of their child's care and all levels of decision making" (p. 19). The issue of parent choice in determining the settings in which services will occur is a critical issue. The IFSP team, like the IEP team, bears the responsibility for determining the appropriate settings in which services should occur. However, there has been some controversy as to the weight of family voice in determining services and placement. According to OSEP (J. Heskett, personal communication, May 26, 1999), the family cannot unilaterally decide the services or location of services provided through Part C:

Although Part C recognizes the importance of, and requires, parent involvement throughout the IFSP process, Part C does not relieve the State lead agency of its responsibility to ensure that other regulatory and statutory requirements, including the natural environments provisions, are met. While the family provides significant input regarding the provision of appropriate early intervention services, ultimate responsibility for determining what services are appropriate for a particular infant or toddler, including the location of such services, rests with the IFSP team as a whole. Therefore, it would be inconsistent with Part C for decisions of the IFSP team to be made unilaterally based solely on preference of the family. The State bears no responsibility under Part C for services that are selected exclusively by the parent; however, the State must still provide all other services on the IFSP for which the parent did consent.

Some individuals have expressed concern that when services are no longer provided in centers, family support and parent-to-parent services are no longer available. Such important family services as needed by a particular family must continue to be included on an IFSP. The setting in which services are received should in no way drive the availability of needed family support. This is clarified in another letter from OSEP (E. Yarnell, personal communication, October 19, 1999):

We share your concerns for the isolation and for the networking and training needs of parents. These are particularly important family needs and should be addressed by the IFSP team as a part of the development of the child's IFSP ....

... any justification for the child's services to take place in a setting other than a natural environment must relate to the child's individual needs. Nothing in the law precludes such services from being provided in settings that include other children with disabilities as well as nondisabled children, as long as the requirements of Part C are met, so that many opportunities may exist for parents of children with disabilities to interact. Because a parent's need for time with other parents of children with disabilities can be successfully accommodated in the natural environments where the child receives services, or in separate meetings, this parent need cannot be used as a justification to deny the child the appropriate services in natural environments ....

... for services directed solely at the parent such as parent support, those services are not required to take place in a "natural environment." No justification, therefore, is needed on the IFSP. Such services solely for the parent, however, cannot be used as a justification for providing services to the child in other than natural environments.

Transition

The transition from early intervention to preschool has been well defined in the literature, as well as provided for in IDEA '97. IDEA requires that a transition meeting and plan be developed at least 90 days and up to six months prior to the child turning three years of age, even if the child will not receive preschool special education services. The family is required to have adequate time to prepare for and develop a transition plan that includes gathering information they need to make decisions about future services.

From an ecological perspective, transition is a change in a person's role, setting, or both, and involves a "process of mutual accommodation" between the child and family and their environments (Bronfenbrenner, 1979, p. 27). Providing services in natural settings recognizes and builds upon the family as nurturer of the physical, economic, and psychosocial functions of the child. Klein and White (1996) propose that, "as the child develops, his or her functions in the family change from mainly being supported and maintained to increasingly symbiotic" (p. 224), all of which is based on the child's development and learning. Therefore, as a child grows and matures, he/she becomes less dependent on the family ecosystem for nurturance. As the child moves from early intervention to the preschool environment, he/she may also expand the amount of time spent outside the family (e.g., going from home to a program or school) affecting the level of direct involvement of the family in the role of direct provider and/or supporter of services.

While natural environments in early intervention are comparable to least restrictive environments or inclusive settings in preschool services, families must be aware of and plan for differences between the early intervention program components and preschool program components. These can include changes in contexts, services, and process. Context refers to the ways in which services are designed. Early intervention services are designed around supporting the needs of the child and the family to promote the child's continuing development. Preschool services are provided based on educational relevance and are provided only if the disability has an adverse effect upon learning. Because of these differences in context, a child may receive more or fewer services when they move to the preschool setting. While many preschool programs also include a family component, the major focus of services is on the child at this level. Finally, there are potential differences in the processes used to determine and provide services (e.g., evaluations, eligibility, procedural safeguards).

In implementing natural environments, several states are including provisions that help families understand the differences in focus and terminology that exist between early intervention services and preschool services offered through the public schools, Head Start or other preschool programs, such as child care agencies. Kentucky has implemented several training initiatives that focus on helping families understand the differences between early intervention services in natural environments and preschool inclusive services. However, states must additionally assist service providers in developing transition outcomes for both the child and family that include identifying community supports that can be used during and after the transition to preschool services, which can further assist the family in developing mechanisms for addressing the needs of the child both within the home environment and in community settings.

Moving Toward the Natural Environments Mandate

Many states have long and successful histories of providing early intervention services. For some, the changes required to implement the natural environments mandate must focus on ensuring that services are provided in environments based on family routines and schedules, and away from having the family always come to a central location for services, especially when centers or clinics provide services to children with disabilities only. For others, they must recognize that the setting alone does not meet the natural environments mandate. They must change the context in which services are provided. For example, arriving at the family's home with a bag of toys and working with the child while the family member is out of the room is not meeting the intent of early intervention services in natural environments.

To assist in facilitating the change from the current service delivery system to one in which services are provided in natural environments, states and local communities are currently developing and implementing policies and practices to support the provision of early intervention services in natural environments. State Part C systems are using a variety of strategies to address the issues and challenges inherent in successfully implementing these policies and practices. Some examples of these are listed below.

Statewide Planning

A number of states (e.g., Washington, Georgia, Nebraska, Kentucky) have established statewide task forces or planning groups to address successful implementation of these requirements. Colorado established the Babies' Early Learning Opportunities Nurture Growth (BELONG) initiative. The purpose of this initiative is to promote supports and services that are: provided in everyday routines, activities, and places, developmentally appropriate, and relevant to families' lives. Activities of the initiative include collaboration at the state level, public awareness, education and training, and local community capacity building.

Training and Technical Assistance

Many states have ongoing statewide training and technical assistance systems to assist all communities in implementing these requirements. For example, Nebraska conducts regional forums across the state, Virginia holds regional trainings for providers and parents, and Missouri sponsors mentoring partnerships.

Written Guidelines

In addition to the states referenced in this article, many state lead agencies and particularly state Interagency Coordinating Councils (ICC) have developed and made available fact sheets, guidelines, manuals, and memoranda. These documents detail the federal requirements, provide state guidance, and offer strategies for successful implementation. For example, the Georgia ICC (1999) published two fact sheets on natural environments. The Virginia Part C system (1999) developed a document on early intervention that, among other things, includes a comparison of their current recommended service delivery practices with more traditional, center-based segregated delivery systems. The New Jersey Early Intervention System (1998) has made available a number of technical assistance documents including a comparison of traditional beliefs and expectations about natural environments and corresponding facts to respond to each. The Nebraska Departments of Education and Health and Human Services (2000) published several fact sheets outlining the principles of recommended practice for services in natural environments. Kentucky is developing a longitudinal self-assessment process and guiding principles based on the state policy statement that will be implemented as part of the state monitoring system. Many states have developed question and answer documents with the most frequently asked questions included.

Regional and Local Planning

States such as New Jersey, Virginia, South Dakota, and Colorado required regional or local early intervention systems to develop and implement interagency plans for the implementation of the requirements. The Kansas Part C System issued a Technical Assistance Bulletin (January, 2000) describing the natural environments requirements and recommending, among other ideas, that local interagency coordinating councils develop and implement strategies to address the challenges in their community. According to the state lead agency, these can include community education and training, collaboration with the broader early childhood community, and encouraging families who have been successful in natural environments to share their experiences with families entering the system.

Funding Incentives

The Missouri First Steps Part C System provides natural environments incentive money to offer additional funding to providers who are traveling into the community to deliver early intervention services. In addition, the Missouri Medicaid program pays a higher rate to providers who travel into community settings. Both the extra Medicaid funding and the First Steps natural environment incentive money is an additional $2.50 per 15 minutes of service.

This list is certainly not exhaustive but provides examples of some approaches being used. To learn more about how states are addressing the natural environments requirements, go to the National Early Childhood Technical Assistance System (NEC*TAS) web site at www.nectas.unc.edu and select *Keys to Inclusion*. It contains information on strategies that some states are using to implement natural environments successfully.

All across the country, state and community planners, families, and providers are working together to implement the IDEA Part C natural environments requirements. Although there are challenges, successes are occurring daily. While changing the context and location in which we are providing early intervention services can be challenging, the results will most surely be positive for young children with disabilities and their families.

Note

Beth Rous can be reached by e-mail at brous@ihdi.uky.edu

References

Assistance to states for the education of children with disabilities, 64 Fed. Reg. 12639 (1999).

Bredekamp, S. & Copple, C. (Eds) (1997). *Developmentally appropriate practice in early childhood programs* (Rev ed.). Washington, DC: National Association for the Education of Young Children.

Bronfenbrenner, U. (1979). *The ecology of human development: Experiments by nature and design.* Cambridge, MA: Harvard College Press.

Connecticut Birth to Three System (1999). *Service guidelines 2 natural environments: Intervention guidance for service providers and families.* Hartford, CT: Connecticut Department of Mental Retardation.

Division for Early Childhood (1993). *DEC recommended practices: Indicators for quality in programs for infants and young children with special needs and their families.* Reston, VA: Division for Early Childhood, Council for Exceptional Children.

Division for Early Childhood (1994). *Personnel standards for early education and early intervention: Guidelines for licensure in early childhood special education.* Washington, DC.

Early Childhood Connections (1999). *A guidebook: Early intervention supports and services in everyday routines, activities, and places in Colorado.* Denver, CO: Early Childhood Connections, Colorado Department of Education and University of Colorado JFK Partners.

Early intervention program for infants and toddlers with disabilities, 34 C.F.R. 303 (1999).

Erwin, E.J. (1996). The promise and challenge of supporting all children in natural environments. In E.J. Erwin (Ed.), *Putting children first: Visions for a brighter future for young children and their families* (pp. 199-224) Baltimore: Paul H. Brookes.

Erwin, E.J. & Schreiber, R. (1999). Creating supports for young children with disabilities in natural environments. *Early Childhood Education Journal, 26*, 167-171.

Georgia State Interagency Coordinating Council (1999). *Frequently asked questions: Natural environments.* Atlanta, GA: Author

IDEA Infant and Toddler Coordinators Association (2000). *Position paper on the provision of early intervention services in accordance with federal requirements on natural environments.*

Kansas Infant-Toddler Services (2000). *Technical assistance bulletin, tab #6.* Topeka, KS: Kansas Department of Health and Environment.

Klein, D.M. & White, J.M. (1996). *Family theories: An introduction.* Thousand Oaks, CA: Sage.

Kleinhammer-Tramill, P.J. & Rosenkoetter, S.E. (1994). Early intervention and secondary/transition services: Harbingers of change in education. *Focus on Exceptional Children, 27*, 1-14.

Missouri Dept. of Elementary and Secondary Education (1999). *First steps technical assistance bulletin - natural environments: Putting principles into practice* [On-line] Available: www.coe.missouri.edu/~mocise/pubs/fsta/2.htm

Nebraska Departments of Education and Health and Human Services (2000). *System of early intervention: Natural environments... where children spend their time* Vol.1. Lincoln, NE: Author

New Jersey Early Intervention System (1998). *Beliefs and expectations: Consider this.* Trenton, NJ: New Jersey Department of Health and Senior Services.

Noonan, M.J. & McCormick, L. (1993). *Early intervention in natural environments: Methods and procedures.* Florence, KY: Wadsworth.

Thurman, S.K. (1997). Systems, ecologies, and the context of early intervention. In S. K. Thurman, J.R. Cornwell, & S.R. Gottwald, (Eds.), *Contexts of early intervention systems and settings* (pp. 3-18). Baltimore: Paul H. Brookes.

Virginia Babies Can't Wait! (1999). *Virginia's family-centered early intervention approach: An overview.* Richmond, VA: Virginia Department of Mental Health, Mental Retardation and Substance Abuse Services.

It's Only Natural...

to Have Early Intervention in the Environments Where It's Needed

---

R. A. McWilliam, Ph.D., University of North Carolina at Chapel Hill

What Are Natural Environments?

In 1997, Congress reauthorized the federal law governing early intervention services with a new twist. Early intervention services are now to be provided in settings where children would be if they were not in early intervention (Individuals with Disabilities Education Amendments, 1997). Simply, this means services should be provided in the home and the community, including child care settings. The purpose of the law is to discourage settings that separate children with disabilities and their families from places and activities that they use if the children did not have disabilities.

Why Are Early Intervention Programs Paying Attention to Natural Environments?

Early intervention programs are paying attention to natural environments, not only because they're in the law, but also because research points out the benefits of doing things "naturalistically" (Hart, 1985; Hepting & Goldstein, 1996; Santos & Lugnugaris-Kraft, 1997; Weisner, Bausano, & Kornfein, 1983). For example, studies have shown that a focus on informal support rather than "parent training" produces successful results in children and families (Allen & Petr, 1996; Cohen & Wills, 1985; Powell, 1987); working with children in their classroom settings (like day care) is better than pulling them out into a therapy or instruction room (McWilliam, 1996); and following children's cues is more effective than is the use of structured drill work (Hemmeter & Kaiser, 1994; Kaiser, Hendrickson, & Alpert, 1991; Warren, 1991).

Note that the research supporting naturalistic interventions has not always studied "natural" versus "unnatural," but has shown that natural interventions can work. Furthermore, there is a large body of evidence that direct instruction works, but this research has involved teachers spending time working directly with children in classrooms. The focus of this paper is on home visits and community interventions, where a teacher or therapist has about an hour of contact with a child per week.

Even though the early intervention field is moving rapidly towards natural environments, many professionals are struggling with the change. They have been used to working with children in self-contained settings, or having families come in for their therapy or instruction sessions, or believing that their hands-on work with children is what makes children improve. The good news is that many states have been using natural environments for a long time; this is not some radical new idea forced upon us by the bureaucrats in Washington. In fact, the bureaucrats adopted the policy because the field told them it was the right way to go.

How Will Services Change?

Many families might be concerned about any changes in their services. Throughout the U.S., the use of natural environments results in certain predictable changes, although each state makes its own decisions about how to interpret the law. If programs follow the intent of the law, the following list shows 10 changes they should probably make.

New Ways of Providing Services

1. At intake, professionals will seek to understand the family's "ecology" (who's involved and what the relationships are like) (Bronfenbrenner, 1986), more than on medical information and providing information about the program.

2. IFSP[a] meetings will focus on routines more than on test results (McWilliam, 1992).

---

[a] Individualized Family Service Plan

3. IFSP outcomes will be developed from needs occurring in the family's routines rather than on tests used for determining current level of functioning (McWilliam, Ferguson, et al., 1998).

4. Services will be decided after outcomes (goals) are decided rather than before.

5. The IFSP team rather than evaluators and referral sources will decide on what services and intensity are needed.

6. Early intervention professionals will work primarily with regular caregivers (parents and child care teachers) rather than children.

7. Families will get at least one home visit a week from one primary service provider (Kochanek & Buka, 1998) rather than home visits from different professionals.

8. Professionals will understand that daily interactions with the child during regular routines are more important for child progress (Gallimore, Weisner, Bernheimer, Guthrie, & Nihira, 1992) than are their sessions with the child.

9. Professionals will coordinate their services through consultation with each other and joint visits (McCormick & Goldman, 1979; Raver, 1991) rather than do their own thing and not learn from each other.

10. Professionals will provide emotional, informational, and material support rather than only instructional support to the child (Davis & Rushton, 1991; Dunst, 1990; Dunst, Trivette, & Hamby, 1996).

What Can Families Do?

The responsibility for making sure early intervention occurs in natural environments belongs to the professional, but there are six things families can do to make sure their early intervention experience is as effective as possible.

1. Examine Their Routines

Functional intervention and the planning that precedes it is based on families' everyday activities (McWilliam, 1992). It also includes those activities that don't happen every day but that are important rituals for families, such as going to religious activities, visiting Grandma, or going to the grocery store. Families can ask themselves whether each of these routines is satisfactory. If not, they can examine what the family does, and then specifically what the child with disabilities does. About the child, they can ask themselves, "How much does he participate in the routine?" "How independent is she?" "How does he get along with other people at this time of day?" Ultimately, the question is "Is this routine working for my family (Bernheimer & Keogh, 1995)? If not, what might make it easier or less stressful?"

2. Do the Math

Families are often tempted to get any service available and to ask for as much of it as possible (McWilliam, Young, & Harville, 1996). It's important to remember that the amount of a service is not what's important, because *all the child's learning occurs between sessions* (McWilliam, 1996). The sessions themselves are only useful for getting information to regular caregivers like family members and child care providers. Unlike special education, where the direct instruction to an *older* child might have some learning benefit, children under the age of 36 months are not going to generalize to noninstructional time. The benefits of direct instruction with infants and young children is not entirely clear, but—even if it were—it would be the caregivers not the itinerant professionals who would be providing such instruction. So the point remains that the purpose of the home visit should not be seen as direct instruction of the child but consultation to the parent. Nick Hobbs (Hobbs et al., 1984) recognized this a long time ago when he exhorted special educators to be consultants to families.

How many sessions a week does it take to give a caregiver suggestions for eating, dressing, playing with toys, sitting independently, or whatever the outcomes for the child are? Unfortunately, some families have been misled into believing that the hands-on time with a specialist (therapist or teacher) is what makes the child progress. It's not. It's the work the family and other people who work with the child do that makes for progress. When parents think the hands-on sessions are effective, however, they of course want as much time as possible. They therefore want 60 minutes of therapy rather than 30 minutes a week.

Wait a minute, though! Remember that the learning occurs between visits. Let's say a therapist is working on independent sitting, holding toys in each hand, and making eye contact with a parent (presumably because the parent wanted the child to be able to play with her). Two sessions of therapy might come to 60 minutes a week. Now let's assume that the caregivers can work on sitting, toy holding, and eye contact during the day. Realistically, they can probably work on these three skills a total of about 10 minutes an hour, on average—some hours more, some hours less. Now let's assume the child is awake from 8:00 until 11:00 A.M. (3 hours), 1:00 until 4:00 P.M. (3 hours), and 6:00 until 10:00 P.M. (4 hours). At 10 minutes of "intervention" an hour, the child is getting a total of 100 minutes a day. Compare this to 60 minutes of therapy a week. Again, consider how often caregivers need specialists to help them implement interventions during natural routines. *The most important lesson for families to remember is that all the learning occurs between sessions.*

3. Make Sure They Get Emotional Support

It's not easy being a parent, especially a parent in early intervention. Parents often get emotional support from their own family, but they also want support from people who are knowledgeable about child development, disabilities, and services (Tocci, McWilliam, & Harbin, 1998; National Association of State Boards of Education, 1991). When families find a family member, friend, or professional who makes them feel competent, confident, and safe, they should treasure that relationship (Crnic, Greenberg, & Slough, 1986).

4. Make Sure They Get Information

Most families want as much information as they can get about their child's disability, services, and what they can do to help their child (Gowen, Christy, & Sparling, 1993). It's important to remember that *not every need requires a service*[b]. Just because the child is delayed in talking, for example, it doesn't mean he needs speech therapy (McWilliam et al., 1996). It's possible that the regular home visitor (who might be a "teacher") and the parents can figure out how to help the child with his talking. Certainly, *parents should be very wary about*

---

[b] P. J. McWilliam (personal communication; date unknown—she said it for years)

having to take their child to therapy or instruction sessions at a clinic, office, or hospital (McWilliam & Strain, 1993). Almost everything that needs to be done with a young child and family can be done in the family's natural environments—and clinics, offices, and hospitals are not natural!

Because the home visit is one of the most critical parts of natural environments, families will need to understand that their role in home visits is to get information. They therefore need to be talking to the home visitor throughout the visit. So they need to stay in the room! (See item 6 under following section, Professionals Will Focus on Support During Home Visits).

5. Make Sure They Get Material Support

It is very hard for a family to do the things they want to do for their child if their basic needs are not being met. If families are suffering from inadequate housing, clothing, food, and so on, they need to ask their service coordinator for help. Service coordinators in early intervention are supposed to be able to direct families to the community resources that can help with these basic needs (Trivette, Dunst, & Deal, 1997).

6. Develop a Relationship With One Primary Service Provider

An important reason not to have too many professionals to deal with is that the greatest strength in early intervention is the relationship between families and their primary service provider (McWilliam et al., 1995). Nurturing a relationship takes energy, although the responsibility in early intervention for doing this belongs to the professional. Nevertheless, if families have to divide their time and emotional energy among too many professionals, it makes it harder to develop one strong bond.

What Should Families Expect From Professionals?

Families can do a lot to take advantage of early intervention occurring in natural environments. But, ultimately, professionals are responsible for making it work. Parents already have a lot to do with their primary responsibility of caring for their child and the rest of the family. Families can therefore have the following six expectations about what professionals will do.

1. Professionals Will Work in the Home and Community

Research and the law encourages services to occur where children and their families would spend time if the child did not have a disability.

2. Professionals Will Find Out About the Family's "Ecology"

To take advantage of families' "natural resources," professionals will want to know about the immediate family, extended family and friends, services, and community resources the family currently uses. Families can give this information at their own discretion.

3. Professionals Will Find Out About the Family's Routines

To help develop a functional IFSP, professionals will want to know about the family's day-to-day life. They will have conversations with families about what the family does in each of their routines. Again, families can tell only as much as they want professionals to know.

4. Professionals Will Support Families to Make Decisions About Services

Even though it might seem scary for families at first, they can make the major decisions about what to work on and how that will happen. But they are not alone; a team of professionals is in place to help. Professionals will help families make decisions about the outcomes on the IFSP and the resources needed to meet those outcomes.

5. Professionals Will Explain How Sometimes Less Is More

Unfortunately, society—including professionals in early intervention—often dupe parents into thinking that more is better. Families are led to believe that (1) every need requires a service and (2) the more sessions or time you get of that service the more effective it will be. We have already explained that needs don't necessarily require formal services. It is true that children need lots of stimulation and, more important, feedback ("reinforcement") that teaches them. But this does not come from instructional or therapy sessions (McWilliam, 1995). This comes from daily interactions with caregivers. So then the questions about services become:

- What service do I really *need* to help other people looking after my child or me accomplish the goals we decided upon?
- If I need a service for this right now, how often do I *need* this consultation?

I believe most families understand that it's best not to use up valuable resources like therapists' time when it's not actually needed. This time is then available to families who do actually need it (McWilliam & Bailey, 1994).

6. Professionals Will Focus on Support During Home Visits

Home visits used to look like little home-school or play-therapy sessions. No more. The child does not learn from home visits—the family does. The purpose of home visits is to ensure that the family has all the support they need to meet their priorities the rest of the week. So, home visitors will encourage family members, listen to them, make sure their basic needs are met, and provide them with information. One way to provide information might be to show them things to do with the child. But such a demonstration or "model" is only one of many ways of supporting families. Most of it is done through talking.

I have described natural environments and explained why early intervention programs are paying attention to them. This will involve some change in the way some programs have done business, and change is difficult. But it's an exciting direction: It makes sense to families, it is backed up by good research, and it should result in better outcomes for children and families. Many states are doing the things described here. Families and professionals can begin this journey hand in hand. They have to.

Note

Dr. Robin McWilliam is the director of Project INTEGRATE at the Frank Porter Graham Child Development Center, University of North Carolina at Chapel Hill.

This article was originally written for parents at the request of one state's Part C staff. The work is funded by an outreach grant from the U.S. Department of Education, Office of Special Education Programs (Grant No. H024D70034). Opinions expressed herein are those of the author and do not necessarily represent the position of the U.S. Department of Education. Appreciation is extended to Lisa Mayhew, Stacy Scott, and Katie Harville for their contributions to this work.

Address correspondence to R. A. McWilliam, Frank Porter Graham Child Development Center, CB#8180, University of North Carolina at Chapel Hill, Chapel Hill, NC 27516-8180. E-mail: Robin_McWilliam@unc.edu.

References

Allen, R.I. & Petr, C.G. (1996). Toward developing standards and measurements for family-centered practice in family support programs. In G.H.S. Singer, L.E. Powers, & A.L. Olson (Eds.), *Redefining family support: Innovations in public-private practice* (pp. 57-85). Baltimore: Paul H. Brookes.

Bernheimer, L.P. & Keogh, B.K. (1995). Weaving interventions into the fabric of everyday life: An approach to family assessment. *Topics in Early Childhood Special Education, 15,* 415-433.

Bronfenbrenner, U. (1986). Ecology of the family as a context for human development: Research perspectives. *Developmental Psychology, 22,* 723-742.

Cohen, S. & Wills, T.A. (1985). Stress, social support, and the buffering hypothesis. *Psychological Bulletin, 98,* 310-357.

Crnic, K.A., Greenberg, M.T., & Slough, N.M. (1986). Early stress and social support influences on mothers' and high-risk infants' functioning in late infancy. *Infant Mental Health Journal, 7,* 19-33.

Davis, H. & Rushton, R. (1991). Counseling and supporting parents of children with developmental delay: A research evaluation. *Journal of Mental Deficiency Research, 35*(2), 89-112.

Dunst, C.J. (1990). Family support principles: Checklists for program builders and practitioners. *Family systems intervention monograph 2*(5). Morganton, NC: Family, Infant and Preschool Program, Western Carolina Center.

Dunst, C.J., Trivette, C.M., & Hamby, D.W. (1996). Measuring the helpgiving practices of human services program practitioners. *Human Relations, 49,* 815-835.

Gallimore, R., Weisner, T.S., Bernheimer, L.P., Guthrie, D., & Nihira, K. (1992). Family responses to young children with developmental delays: Accommodation activity in ecological and cultural context. *American Journal on Mental Retardation, 98,* 185-206.

Gowen, J.W., Christy, D.S., & Sparling, J. (1993). Informational needs of parents of young children with special needs. *Journal of Early Intervention, 17,* 194-210.

Hart, B. (1985). Naturalistic language training techniques. In S.F. Warren & A.K. Rogers-Warren (Eds.), *Teaching functional language* (pp. 63-88). Austin, TX: Pro-Ed.

Hemmeter, M.L. & Kaiser, A.P. (1994). Enhanced milieu teaching: Effects of parent-implemented language intervention. *Journal of Early Intervention, 18,* 269-289.

Hepting, N.H. & Goldstein, H. (1996). What's natural about naturalistic language intervention? *Journal of Early Intervention, 20,* 250-265.

Hobbs, N., Dokecki, P.R., Hoover-Dempsey, K.V., Moroney, R.M., Shayne, M.W., & Weeks, K.H. (1984). *Strengthening families.* San Francisco: Jossey Bass.

Individuals with Disabilities Education Amendments of 1997, PL 105-17. U.S. *Statutes at Large, 108.*

Kaiser, A.P., Hendrickson, J.M., & Alpert, C.L. (1991). Milieu language teaching: A second look. *Advances in Mental Retardation and Developmental Disabilities, 4,* 63-92.

Kochanek, T.T. & Buka, S.L. (1998). Patterns of early intervention service utilization: Significant child, maternal, and service provider factors. *Journal of Early Intervention, 21,* 217-231.

McCormick, L. & Goldman, R. (1979). The transdisciplinary model: Implications for service delivery and personnel preparation for the severely and profoundly handicapped. *AAESPH Review, 4,* 152-161.

McWilliam, R.A. (1992). *Family-centered intervention planning: A routines-based approach.* Tucson, AZ: Communication Skill Builders, Inc. (now available only from author).

McWilliam, R.A. (1995). Integration of therapy and consultative special education: A continuum in early intervention. *Infants and Young Children, 7*(4), 29-38.

McWilliam, R.A. (Ed.) (1996). *Rethinking pull-out services in early intervention: A professional resource.* Baltimore: Paul H. Brookes.

McWilliam, R.A. & Bailey, D.B., Jr. (1994). Predictors of service-delivery models in center-based early intervention. *Exceptional Children, 61,* 56-71.

McWilliam, R.A., Ferguson, A., Harbin, G.L., Porter, P., Munn, D., & Vandiviere, P. (1998). The family-centeredness of individualized family service plans. *Topics in Early Childhood Special Education, 18,* 69-82.

McWilliam, R.A., Lang, L., Vandiviere, P., Angell, R., Collins, L., & Underdown, G. (1995). Satisfaction and struggles: Family perceptions of early intervention services. *Journal of Early Intervention, 19,* 43-60.

McWilliam, R.A. & Strain, P.S. (1993). Service delivery models. In Task Force on Recommended Practices, Division for Early Childhood, Council for Exceptional Children, *DEC recommended practices: Indicators of quality in programs for infants and young children with special needs and their families* (pp. 40-49). Reston, VA: Council for Exceptional Children.

McWilliam, R.A., Young, H.J., & Harbin, G. (1996). Therapy services in early intervention: Current status, barriers, and recommendations. *Topics in Early Childhood Special Education, 16,* 348-374.

National Association of State Boards of Education (1991). *Caring communities: Supporting young children and families.* Alexandria, VA: Author.

Powell, D.R. (1987). Life in a parent support program: Research perspectives. *Family Resource Coalition Report, 6*(3), 4-5, 18.

Raver, S.A. (1991). *Strategies for teaching at-risk and handicapped infants and toddlers: A transdisciplinary approach.* New York: Macmillan.

Santos, R.M. & Lugnugaris-Kraft, B. (1997). Integrating research on effective instruction with instruction in the natural environment for young children with disabilities. *Exceptionality, 7,* 97-129.

Tocci, L., McWilliam, R.A., & Harbin, G.L. (1998). Family-centered services: Service providers' discourse and behavior. *Topics in Early Childhood Special Education, 18,* 206-221.

Trivette, C., Dunst, C., & Deal, A. (1997). Resource-based early intervention practices. In S.K. Thurman, J.R. Cornwell, & S.R. Gottwald (Eds.), *The contexts of early intervention: Systems and settings* (pp. 73-92). Baltimore: Paul H. Brookes.

Warren, S.F. (1991). Enhancing communication and language development with milieu teaching procedures. In E. Cipani (Ed.), *A guide for developing language competence in preschool children with severe and moderate handicaps* (pp. 68-93). Springfield, IL: Charles C. Thomas.

Weisner, T.S., Bausano, M., & Kornfein, M. (1983). Putting family ideas into practice: Pronaturalism in conventional and non-conventional California families. *Ethos, 11,* 278-304.

Expanding the Circle of Inclusion

The Child Care Director's Role

Susan Craig, Ph.D., AGH Associates, Inc.
Ann Haggart, Ed.M., AGH Associates, Inc.
Susan Gold, Ed.D., Mailman Center for Child Development
Karla Hull, Ph.D., Associate Professor, College of Education
Valdosta State University

Introduction

Despite federal and state laws that require services in the least restrictive environment, as well as research which supports its benefits, broad based implementation of inclusive child care continues to elude us (Brown, 1997). Early interventionists trained to address the needs of infants and toddlers with disabilities within formal, planned learning opportunities struggle with the more informal, open-ended structure of center-based child care programs (Bruder & Dunst, 1999). Child care directors, although aware of the Americans with Disabilities mandate to make both public and private child care programs accessible to children with disabilities, are not well informed about the need for child care among the families of young children with disabilities (Craig, 1996; Craig & Haggart, 1994). As a result, only a small percentage of families seeking inclusive child care are able to find it (Devore & Hanley-Maxwell, 2000; Fewell, 1993; Gold, 2000; Guralnick, 2000; Landis, 1992).

Until recently, most efforts to promote inclusive child care have primarily focused on child care *providers*. Since providers are responsible for the day-to-day care of children, training on atypical development and the accommodations necessary for caring for children with disabilities is directed at them. While this type of training is important, it tends to ignore the important role child care *directors* play in setting program policies. Child care directors are in the position of either encouraging or discouraging the enrollment of children with disabilities. They represent a previously untapped resource for solving the problem of inclusive child care.

Much like a principal of a school, the child care director's vision inspires the kind of care available at a center. Research on educational change and effectiveness consistently points to the role of the program administrator as having a critical influence on making programmatic and policy changes (Berman & McLaughlin 1978; Fullan, 1991; Rutter et al., 1979; Sergiovanni, 1994). In fact, program level administrators are the people "most likely to be in a position to shape the organizational conditions necessary for success, such as the development of

shared goals, collaborative work structures and climates, and procedures for monitoring results" (Fullan, 1991, p. 76). Child care directors determine center policies, as well as procedures for enrollment and dismissal (Bloom, 1988). They are responsible for training providers, setting program standards, and modeling quality care for other employees (Bloom & Sheere, 1992). Given the scope of their responsibility and power, collaboration between early intervention and child care directors is an important step in creating center policies which encourage the participation of young children with disabilities.

You have to start with the directors. We learned that first hand. There was a statewide training for providers ... they went back to their centers and many were not allowed to practice what they had learned because the director didn't have the same information or philosophy. (Child Care Director, Morgantown, WV, 1998)

The directors are the ones who ultimately allow us access to their center, so it is essential that we get them on board and develop positive relationships with them. (Early Interventionist, Temple, TX, 1998)

Getting Directors on Board

For the past several years, the authors have worked with the directors of 52 child care programs in Alabama, Massachusetts, Maryland, New Hampshire, Texas, West Virginia, and the American Virgin Islands through federally funded model demonstration and outreach projects. The project's goal is to provide Part C coordinators in each participating state with an easily replicated model for partnering with child care directors to create accessible child care options for infants and toddlers with disabilities. Easy replication was assured through the use of inexpensive, self-paced training materials, along with the state Part C's financial commitment to support the collaboration between early intervention and the child care community.

All of the participating project child care directors attended 24 hours of training on inclusion and revised their programs policies and procedures to reflect a commitment to inclusive child care. The majority of the directors worked with local Part C personnel to complete an additional 30 hours of inclusion activities. At the conclusion of these training activities the directors and Part C personnel took part in individual telephone interviews conducted by a professional who was not associated with the training. The interviews were designed to assist in evaluating the quality of training offered to the directors and the impact of this training on the staff and children in their programs. Excerpts from the interviews appear throughout the text.

The directors were overwhelmingly supportive of the training. Now firmly committed to inclusive child care, the child care directors offer Part C early intervention programs the following suggestions:

Define Child Care's Role

Enthusiasm for inclusive child care grows as directors learn to appreciate the contribution their programs can make to children with disabilities and their families. Be sure to take every opportunity to let child care directors know what a vital resource they can be. Recognize the important role personal experience plays in making a commitment to inclusive child care. Reach out to the child care directors in your community and encourage them to meet with other directors who are already enrolling infants and toddlers with disabilities.

> *I had my misgivings in the beginning, I'll admit it. But I had some providers willing to "give it a go," so I decided to try it. We enrolled several children with disabilities. And it was amazing. The providers started coming to me saying "You've got to see Germain!" "You won't believe what Jorge is doing!" The one that really stands out in my mind is a little boy with spina bifida. When he enrolled he could neither walk or talk. But now he can walk. He dances and sings. It's just incredible to be a part of something like this. (Child Care Director, Maryland, 1993)*

Let directors know that you value their years of experience with children. Scaffold new information about the care of infants and toddlers with disabilities onto what they already know. Support their efforts to link the need for inclusive child care to other beliefs they hold about the best program for children in their care.

After listening to how age appropriate routines could help a child with disabilities, I went back to my center and changed the placements of two of our children. We had kept both children in the infant room even though they were older. We were worried about them being with older children before they had learned how to walk. But in my heart, it didn't feel right. I knew those children could do more than we were asking them to. So when I heard about the importance of age appropriate placements, I got my courage up. And it worked. Those children are doing just fine. (Child Care Director, Waco, TX, 1999)

Recognize the efforts some child care directors have already made to individualize care to meet the needs of the families they serve. If a family has several children already enrolled, it is not unusual for the director to take a sibling born with a disability. Praise the directors who individualize care for children with special needs. Encourage them to share their strategies for helping providers accommodate to these children.

We came to change our minds and what we were doing as we began to see that children with disabilities could be successful in our programs. (Child Care Director, Massachusetts, 1998)

I learned how narrow minded I was about ... incorporating these children into the group environment. I never realized how easy it would be to accommodate and make someone with special needs a part of my center. (Child Care Director, Katy, TX, 1999)

Link Inclusion to Other Efforts at Promoting Quality Care.

All child care directors are concerned with improving the quality of care in their centers. They need to know how inclusive child care can support their efforts to promote quality care. Approach collaboration with early intervention as a way for directors to promote best practices for all children. For example, encourage early intervention staff to use their time to build the capacity of classroom staff to address the language and motor needs of all children enrolled at the center. Rather than discussing child development within the paradigm of clinical milestones, show directors how the early intervention staff coming into their centers can use their knowledge to help classroom staff create and sustain a developmentally appropriate curriculum. Rather than emphasizing the differences between children with disabilities and their typical peers, scaffold information about disabilities onto existing staff competencies and knowledge base.

> *I have learned how to approach child care staff differently. I now look at what they are doing and try to find ways to modify these(activities). I have learned to ... work with their styles rather than impose my own. (Early Interventionist, Temple, TX, 1998)*

Use the Incentives of Staff Training, Funding Options

Child care directors are always looking for ways to fund staff training. This is an area where early intervention can really help child care achieve its goals. Part C coordinators working with this project designated regional service coordinators to serve as "EI Bridges" to local child care programs. Time to collaborate with the directors and assist them in training their providers became one of the services Part C offered to child care through the EI Bridge.

Other funding options you may want to discuss with directors include Child Development Block Grant monies or local charities which support education. Many states now require providers to complete Child Development Associate (CDA) training. Find out who offers that training in your community and offer to co-teach some of the sessions, supplementing the required content with applications for children with disabilities.

> *Discussing financial concerns with early intervention and finding out about alternative funding streams was very helpful. (Child Care Director, West Virginia, 1998)*

Supporting Directors to Stay Involved

Develop Relationships

The shift to inclusive child care involves a process of systemic change for both child care and early intervention. Since the process is difficult for everyone, it is important that the professionals involved in it have the support of one another. To achieve this, the child care directors we worked with recommend that local child care and early intervention programs create a structure for ongoing collaboration. For some programs this might be a monthly brown bag lunch session where common concerns are discussed and common resources shared. For others, the local AEYC chapter could create a subcommittee that serves as a "watch dog" group, which monitors local efforts to support inclusive care. Regardless of the format it takes, the relationship forged between child care directors and early intervention needs to be characterized by respect, mutuality, and a formal system of communication which keeps the vision of inclusion alive.

We have to work hard to build a relationship. I think the early intervention folks thought that child care providers weren't professional enough. They were very territorial in the beginning. However, our partnership is a natural one, once we get past the prejudices. EI has a great rapport with families and so do we. (Child Care Director, Massachusetts, 1998)

Point out Potential Problems

Commitment to inclusive child care requires directors to carefully review program policies and procedures. This is important both in terms of eliminating expectations of behavior or placement, which discriminate against children with disabilities, as well as creating procedures that facilitate these children's smooth enrollment and participation.

Most policies are just as applicable to children with disabilities as they are to more typical peers. These include safety plans which specify procedures for emergency evacuation and regularly scheduled environmental audits to make sure that play areas meet standards for the children's ages and activity levels.

Accommodations for children with disabilities may simply be a more stringent implementation of these rules or minor adjustments based on child specific needs. For example, a four-year-old child with a developmental disability may continue to display mouthing behaviors more common among two-year olds. Strict adherence to the Universal Health Precautions would be important in that four-year old's classroom.

There are, however, some procedures that unintentionally limit the participation of children with disabilities. Rules which prohibit bringing food from home limit the participation of children on special diets; acquisition of certain developmental milestones as a criteria for moving into an age appropriate group is a problem for children who will never be toilet trained or able to walk; dismissal for behavior at the discretion of the director reduces the possibility of working with the family and early intervention provider to implement behavior plans addressing a child's specific problems.

Offer to review a center's policies to identify areas of concern. Suggest ways of rewriting, which make the policies more inclusive. For example, suggest that a statement giving the director the right to dismiss children for behavior be replaced with "when appropriate, the director will meet with the child's parents and a member of his early intervention team to develop and implement a behavior management plan which will help him participate successfully in the center's program." Qualify restrictions about bringing food from home with a statement such as "No food can be brought from home, unless the child has dietary restrictions which require it."

We always had a policy about not moving children into the next classroom, like preschool, until they were potty trained and could walk. (Now I know) that some of them may never be potty trained or walk but that they still belong in age appropriate classrooms. We changed the policy and it is working fine. And for some of the children who weren't potty trained, just being with other children who are potty trained has taught/motivated them to get trained. Now they move on with their peers and it makes a great difference. (Child Care Director, Morgantown, WV, 1998)

I think one of the biggest changes for them (directors) was being asked to put children with disabilities into classrooms by chronological age rather than developmental age classrooms. This was a big change ... but they are doing it. (Early Interventionist, Waco, TX, 1998)

A program policy which requires a visit by the parent and child prior to the first day of attendance is a good way to avoid a situation where a child with disabilities will suddenly show up without any opportunity for the necessary training and/or accommodations to occur. Help directors see that this type of policy gives them time to meet with the family and other members of the IFSP team to make necessary accommodations and schedule necessary training prior to the child's first day.

Waiting lists are another issue to think about as directors move to inclusive care. Some centers find that a dual waiting list, one for children with disabilities, one for children with typical developmental expectations, is an equitable way to provide spaces for all children, while at the same time maintaining an appropriate ratio of children with and without disabilities throughout the center. As in the case of school placements, most child care programs find that following the principle of natural proportions is the best way to maintain successful inclusion. That is, directors accept any child with a disability who is a natural part of the "neighborhood, zone, or district from which the ... (center) draws its ... (children)" (Stainbeck, Stainbeck, & Jackson 1992, p. 13).

Active Recruitment

Let child care directors know what they can do to make the families of children with disabilities feel welcome at their centers. Generic nondiscrimination statements are not enough. Parents need additional reassurance that the center is prepared to offer the support needed for a child with significant disabilities (MacTavish, 1995).

Some directors find asking questions about disabilities right on the enrollment form sets the right tone. For example, "Does your child have a disability or a special need which may require some accommodations to child care activities? If so, please describe so that we can make our program accessible to your child." "Does your child have an IFSP? If so, who is the contact person (name and phone number—release of information is also needed)."

Brochures and enrollment forms should state: "Our center welcomes children with disabilities. In order to properly care for your child we might need additional information or help with making sure we have the support we need. If your child has a disability, please arrange to speak to the director so that we can move the enrollment process quickly along." Statements and procedures like these help the director balance the need to make sure that the child is enrolled in a timely manner with the need for baseline information/training for the provider.

Provide Wrap Around Technical Assistance

Child care directors are busy people, often struggling to retain staff, meet payroll, and stay on top of the many details that go into running a quality program. Acknowledge this by offering to have brief, regularly scheduled meetings with them to monitor the progress of individual children. Use these meetings to discuss ways early intervention services can build the capacity of classroom staff to increase the successful participation of all children. Technical assistance delivered in this manner is aligned with the director's primary goal of providing quality care for all children.

I notice that when I go into the centers [now] ... the staff are asking many more questions about serving the kids .... they seem to be using us as resources and supports in ways that they weren't doing before. (Early Interventionist, Temple, TX, 1998)

Share Your Rolodex

Support for inclusive child care is more forthcoming when child care directors have resources they know they can tap into when a child with disabilities enrolls. The more familiar they are with local medical and community resources, the easier it will be for them to schedule staff training and relieve staff concerns around the care of specific children. Let them know they can count on you. Invite child care directors to training sessions addressing the needs of high-risk children and their families. Nominate them for advisory committees of agencies committed to the care of people with disabilities. Provide them with opportunities to visit the neonatal unit of your local hospital and learn first hand what that environment is like. The more child care directors become part of the early intervention network, the greater the chances of providing seamless services to children with disabilities and their families.

When child care directors become more aware of the EI resources available to them, they are much more willing to accept a child with a disability into their program because they know they will have support .... I now have many more calls from child care directors asking questions or looking for resources for a specific child. (Early Interventionist, Parkersburg, WV, 1998)

Conclusions

Although inclusion of young children with disabilities in neighborhood child care centers has been an ongoing topic in the field, the practice of inclusion lags behind the rhetoric. Child care directors are an untapped resource in changing this situation. We have discussed several ways child care directors can help, as well as strategies to help support their efforts. These include integrating training on the care of children with disabilities into efforts to promote quality care for all children, modifying center policies and procedures, and actively recruiting children with disabilities and their families. Early intervention can support the director's efforts through ongoing wrap around technical assistance, sharing the resources of the early intervention network, and the formation of strong, mutually beneficial relationships. *The directors really do need an EI person to talk to and ask questions and use as a support ... and directors can teach EI folks about the realities of child care ... and what kinds of activities are not effective in child care settings. We can learn from each other. (Child Care Director, Morgantown, WV, 1998)*

Note

Susan Craig can be reached at: craigsus@juno.com

This manuscript was developed as part of an Early Education Program for Children with Disabilities (EEPCD) Outreach project "Successful Integration of Infants and Toddlers with Disabilities" funded by the U.S. Department of Education, Office of Special Education Programs (Grant #HO24D70044-98). The opinions expressed do not necessarily reflect the opinions or policies of the funding agency.

References

Berman, P. & McLaughlin, M. (1978). Implementation of educational innovation. *Educational Forum, 40* (3), 345-370.

Bloom, P.J. (1988, November). *The training and qualifications of child care directors.* Paper Presented at the National Conference in Support of Children and Families. Washington, D.C.

Bloom, P.J. & Sheere, M. (1992). The effect of leadership training on child care program quality. *Early Childhood Research Quarterly, 1,* 579-594.

Brown, W.H. (1997). Inclusion: A time to include and support young children. *Dimensions of Early Childhood, 25,* 3-5.

Bruder, M. & Dunst, C. (1999). Expanding opportunities for infants and toddlers in natural environments: A chance to reconceptualize early intervention. *Zero to Three, 20*(3), 34-36.

Craig, S.E. & Haggart, A.G. (1994). Including all children: The ADA's challenge to early intervention. *Infants and Young Children, 7*(2), 15-19.

Craig, S.E. (1996). Child care centers. In S.K. Thurman, J.R. Cornwell, & S.R. Gottweld (Eds.), *Contexts of early intervention: Systems and settings* (pp. 191-199). Baltimore: Paul H. Brookes.

Devore, S. & Hanley-Maxwell, C. (2000). I wanted to see if we could make it work: Perspctives on inclusive child care. *Exceptional Children, 66*(2), 241-255.

Fewell, R.R. (1993). Child care for children with special needs. *Pediatrics, 91,* 193-198.

Fullan, M. (1991). *The new meaning of educational change.* Teachers College Press.

Gold, S. (2000). Including young children with special needs in early childhood programs: Where is Florida headed? *Children Our Concern,* 23-30.

Guralnick, M.J. (2000). The early intervention system and out of home child care. In D. Cyres & T. Harms (Eds.), *Infants and toddlers in out-of-home care* (pp. 207-234). Baltimore, MD: Paul H. Brookes.

Landis, L.J. (1992). Marital, employment, and child care status of mothers with infants and toddlers with disabilities. *Topics in Early Childhood Special Education, 12,* 496-507.

MacTavish, J. (1995). Focusing on families as a point of service. In S.J. Schleien, J.E. Rynders, L.A. Heyne, & C.E.S. Tabourne (Eds.), *Powerful partnerships: Parents and professionals building inclusive recreation programs together* (pp. 16-18). Minneapolis: The College of Education, University of Minnesota.

Rutter, M., Maughan, B., Mortimore, P., Ouston, J., & Smith, A. (1979). *Fifteen thousand hours.* Cambridge, MA: Harvard University Press.

Sergiovanni, T. (1994). Building community in schools. San Francisco, CA: Jossey-Bass.

Stainbeck, S., Stainbeck, W., & Jackson, H.J. (1992). Toward inclusive classrooms. In S. Stainbeck & W. Stainbeck (Eds.), *Curriculum considerations in inclusive classrooms* (pp. 3-18). Baltimore: Paul H. Brookes.

Interest-Based Natural Learning Opportunities

Carl J. Dunst, Ph.D., Orelena Hawks Puckett Institute, and Family, Infant and Preschool Program, Western Carolina Center
Serena Herter, B.S., Orelena Hawks Puckett Institute
Holly Shields, M.S., Allegheny Singer Research Institute

Many things influence the kinds of learning opportunities children experience. Where a child and family live often determines learning opportunities (Dunst, Bruder, Trivette, Raab, & McLean, 1998). Children living near the ocean may spend lots of time at the beach—playing in the sand, swimming in the ocean, and filling a bucket with water and dumping it into a hole the child has dug in the sand. Children living in cities often get the chance to visit the city zoo, go to children's concerts, and have hands-on science experiences at a science center. Living near a forest or woods provides children opportunities to take nature walks, collect stones and leaves, chase butterflies, and climb on rocks.

Parenting beliefs about desired behavior also influence children's learning opportunities (Gauvain, 1999). Parents with strong religious beliefs are likely to involve their children in different kinds of faith-based activities such as attending religious services, saying grace at family meals, and going to Sunday school. Sports-minded parents are likely to introduce their children to activities such as T-ball, soccer, swimming, or karate classes. Parents who are achievement-oriented are likely to encourage their children's participation in activities emphasizing lessons and skill development such as dance or movement classes, music lessons, and art classes.

Some of the most important determinants of learning opportunities are children's interests and preferences, and strengths and capabilities (Chen, Krechevsky, Viens, & Isberg, 1998; Guberman, 1999). Children who enjoy water often are provided opportunities to express their interests by engaging in backyard water activities, watering plants and flowers, going to the community swimming pool, and splashing in puddles of water after a rain shower. Interests in music and dance often are translated into learning opportunities such as going to children's concerts, taking dancing lessons, playing songs on a jukebox, playing ring-around-the-rosy at a play group, and playing musical instruments at a children's festival. Children who enjoy being around other children often are involved in activities like gym classes, baby swimming classes, neighborhood play groups, little league sports, and going to parties and other social gatherings.

Research and practice show that children's learning and development occurs rapidly when their interests engage them in social and nonsocial activities providing them opportunities to practice existing skills, explore their environments, and learn new abilities (Chen et al., 1998; Dunst, 2000; Gelman, Massey, & McManus, 1991; LeeKeenan & Nimmo, 1993; Mandler, 2000; Nelson, 1999). Nelson (1999), for example, found that variations in child competence were "related easily to the child's life activities and interests" (p. 2). According to Guberman (1999), "children's own interest and sense-making processes [are] a central formulation of supportive environments" (p. 207).

Background

Procedures for identifying children's interests and using them to engage children in community-based learning opportunities are described in this paper. They were developed as part of a model-demonstration project for children with disabilities or delays from birth to 8 years of age and their parents. The purpose of the project was to promote participation in community-based activities and settings as sources of natural learning opportunities (Umstead, Boyd, & Dunst, 1995).

Children's involvement in community-based, natural learning opportunities was evaluated in terms of the characteristics of activities that encouraged participation and the benefits that were gained from the learning opportunities (Bronfenbrenner, 1992). Observations of children participating in community activities, case studies, and surveys of parents and community members were used

Exhibit A

DENNIS THE MENACE

"DO YOU WANT ME TO BEHAVE, OR TO HAVE FUN?"

DENNIS THE MENACE © used by permission of Hank Ketcham and © by North America Syndicate.

to identify the person and environmental characteristics of successful learning activities and opportunities (see especially Dunst, in press). Learning opportunities were considered successful if they were fun and enjoyable and provided a context for expression of both existing and emerging competence as opposed to just compliance (see Exhibit A). Participation in activities that matched and built on children's interests was consistently found to be associated with positive child, parent, and family benefits (Dunst, 2000, in press).

Findings from our analyses of competency-producing community learning activities were used to develop the model shown in Figure 1 (Dunst, 2000). People, objects, and events that interest children are the things that "get their attention" (Fogel, 1997) and encourage them to play, explore, and participate in interactions with people and objects (Göncü, Tuermer, Jain, & Johnson, 1999). Interest-based playing, exploring, and participation is called engagement (McWilliam & Ware, 1994). When children are engaged in everyday activities, they are able to practice existing capabilities and learn new skills (Farver, 1999). Expression of existing and emerging competence is influenced, in part, by how parents and practitioners respond to children's display of competence (e.g., Field, 1978; Rogoff, Mistry, Göncü, & Mosier, 1993; Wolery & Sainato, 1996). As children come to understand the relationship between their behavior and its consequences, their sense of mastery is strengthened (MacTurk & Morgan, 1995). This in turn is likely to reinforce existing interests as well as promote new interests, setting the cycle of influence shown in Figure 1 in motion once again.

Figure 1: Community Learning Opportunities as a Context for Expressing Child Interest and Competence

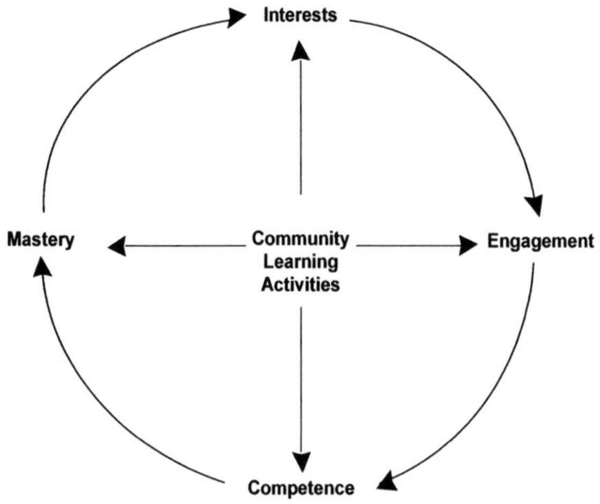

"Suzie," a 2-1/2-year-old child with cerebral palsy, especially liked music. Whether standing or sitting, she "bounced" up and down whenever music was played at home, in the car, or at the mall. Her mother called this "dancing." Suzie's interest in music was used to identify community activities that provided opportunities to express her interest and to display competence (standing without support, singing, "dancing," walking, etc.). One activity was a community music/dance/gymnastics program. Suzie was intent on doing whatever the other children were doing. Walking on a balance beam while making arm movements in concert with music was one of these activities. At first, Suzie held onto two instructors' hands (one on either side of the balance beam) in order to make her way down the balance beam. As she became more competent and "sure of herself" (confident), she began to let go of the instructors' hands and started to make arm movements to the music like the other children. The very first time she traversed the balance beam on her own, Suzie radiated a sense of enjoyment, success, and mastery (she smiled, got excited, and communicated nonverbally "I did it").

Interest-Based Learning Opportunities

Involving children in community learning opportunities that are interest-based involves three steps: (1) identifying children's interests; (2) identifying community activities that provide opportunities for expressing those interests; and (3) involving children in learning opportunities that promote the flow of influence shown in Figure 1. Dunst, Herter, Shields, and Bennis (in press) describe methods and procedures for compiling information about sources of community-based learning activities that can be matched to children's interests.

Identifying Children's Interests

Several different kinds of procedures are available for identifying young children's interests (Chen et al., 1998; Krechevsky, 1998; Moss, 1997). LeeKeenan and Nimmo (1993) noted that child-initiated and child-directed learning "begins with careful observation of children's interests, questions, and ideas and then develops those ideas into concrete learning experiences ... rich in possibilities for varied activity" (pp. 254-255). Observation of children's interests, abilities, and assets—individually and collectively—is a simple but powerful tool for identifying likes and preferences and the kinds of activities that provoke expression of interests. According to Chen et al. (1998), "when a child discovers an area of strength, enjoys exploring it, and feels good about him- or herself, the experience of being successful gives the child the confidence" (p. 63) to express strengths and abilities.

Moss (1997) describes a useful interest-based assessment process for infants, toddlers, preschoolers, and older children. *The Child Preference Indicators* scale includes sets of questions for identifying:

- Preference indicators that identify a child's *favorites*;
- Emotion indicators that focus on a child's *feelings*;
- Socialization indicators that identify a child's *social world and relationships*;
- Self-determination indicators that focus on *child choices*; and
- Physical indicators that identify body *rhythms*.

Table 1 shows the portion of the *Child Preference Indicators* scale used to identify a child's favorite activities, places, and times of the day. An assessment of favorites provides a basis for identifying interests, determining what is engaging to a child, and involving the child in interactions that provide contexts for expressing interests.

Table 1: Questions for Identifying Children's Favorite Places, Objects, and Events

Preferences Indicators FAVORITES			
What are your child's favorites? How can you tell? Do you know why?			
Outside	Foods	Games	Toys
Inside	Music	Smells	Touch, smooth, rough, etc.
Friend	Words	Sounds	Clothes
Structure	Being alone	Crowds	Being read to
Nonstructure	Being sung to	Activities	Place to go
Daytime	Movement	TV show	Animals
Nighttime	Color	Time of day	
Other favorites?_____			

From J. Moss (1997). *The child preference indicators*. Oklahoma City, OK: University Affiliated Program of Oklahoma. Reproduced with permission.

We used a simple but effective procedure for identifying children's interests in the model-demonstration project described earlier. The questions listed in Table 2 were used to assess child affect, engagement, persistence, and competence in different places, routines, and activities and with different toys, materials, and people. The answers to the questions proved especially enlightening in terms of capturing a child's interests, strengths, and assets.

Table 2: Questions for Identifying Children's Interests and Strengths

- What makes the child smile and laugh?

- What makes the child happy and feel good?

- What kinds of things get the child excited?

- What are the child's favorite things to do?

- What things are particularly enjoyable and interesting to the child?

- What does the child especially work hard at doing?

- What gets and keeps the child's attention?

- What is the child especially good at doing?

- What behaviors does the child particularly like to do?

- What "brings out the best" in the child?

- What gets the child to try new things?

The *outcome* of an interest assessment is a *profile* of a child's abilities, strengths, assets, and preferences that collectively characterize his or her *interests*. The assessment itself can be very informal. Noticing that an infant prefers to be in an upright position and bounced up-and-down is an interest-based observation. Taking note that a toddler likes climbing into cabinets and onto a couch or chair is also an interest-based assessment. Experience from our model-demonstration project (Umstead et al., 1995) showed that parents were especially good at recognizing, noticing, and knowing their children's interests. Parents were also good at involving their children in activities that provided opportunities for expressing interests.

Community Learning Opportunities

Armed with information about a child's interests, the next step is to explore options that provide opportunities for expressing those interests. Community-based learning opportunities that offer inclusion experiences (Beckman et al., 1998) and everyday natural learning environments (Dunst & Bruder, 1999) are major sources of these kinds of experiences. These procedures are equally applicable to everyday family life (Dunst & Hamby, 1999) and early childhood programs (Chen et al., 1998; LeeKeenan & Nimmo, 1993).

The procedure for identifying potential sources of community-based learning opportunities as contexts for expressing interests, displaying competence, and learning new abilities is as straightforward as that used for assessing child interests. Taking interests one at a time, a list of possible learning opportunities is generated for the child's immediate and extended community. We accomplish this in collaboration with parents by querying the informational database compiled using the mapping procedures described in Dunst et al. (in press). Why this approach? Because experience tells us that communities are exceedingly rich in potential learning opportunities (Dunst, in press), and  that parents and practitioners cannot possibly remember or invoke all potential learning activities from memory alone.

For example, a child's interests may include playing with, throwing, and kicking balls. Querying an informational database (as well as "thinking about" places and activities that provide opportunities to express this interest) might produce activities such as playgrounds, T-ball, soccer, ball pits, bowling, "playing catch," and kickball. Likewise, assume a child's interests included listening to stories and having books read aloud. Activities and places that might be potential sources of learning opportunities are libraries, library story times, bookstores, bookstore story times, children's plays, storytellers, and drama classes. Idea generation is the goal of this step. The outcome is a potential list of community activities that can provide opportunities for expressing interests.

Participation in Community Activities

Involving children in community learning opportunities that are interest-based is accomplished by choosing those activities that best match child preferences and strengths. This is a little more involved than might at first seem to be the case. Several lessons learned help guide the process of choosing activities for an individual child to increase the likelihood that participation will be successful.

Evidence from our research indicates that birth to six-year-old children's type of participation in community activities varies according to age (Dunst, Hamby, Trivette, Raab, & Bruder, 2000). Simply stated, infant and toddler participation in community activities is often, but not always, more informal and nonstructured. In such instances the characteristics of  settings, and people within settings, provide a basis for expressing interests (e.g., visiting a bookstore where a storyteller engages a child through hand and body movements and voice inflection that the child finds interesting). In contrast, older children's participation tends to be more formal and goal-directed (e.g., attending twice-a-week karate lessons). Experience tells us that chronologically and developmentally younger children's participation in community learning activities is more likely to be successful when opportunities are initially more informal and nonstructured. Learning opportunities often become more structured as children become more capable and competent.

Whether or not a child has previously participated in community activities matters in terms of the choice of learning opportunities. When a child has had few or no community-based learning opportunities, the likelihood of success is increased if you involve the child in *low demand* activities. For example, if a child likes kicking balls, but has little or no experience with any type of group learning opportunity, taking the child to a ball field and just kicking a ball around will probably work better than starting out with soccer lessons. Similarly, if a child likes playing in water, going to a community pool just to play in the water might be more successful than enrolling the child in swimming classes.

The *degree of freedom* of activities also matters a great deal if participation is likely to be fun, enjoyable, and successful. Activities having a low degree of freedom require children to produce specific behavior; whereas, activities with a high degree of freedom provide lots of opportunities for expressing interests.

A 3-1/2-year-old girl we worked with loved art activities and was enrolled in a summer art camp. During the first week of camp, an art instructor encouraged the child to express her interest by mixing colors, painting bold strokes, and expressing herself through painting. The little girl had a wonderful time. The second week, another art instructor insisted that the child "paint in the lines." The girl was miserable and dejected.

The value and importance of serendipitous learning opportunities needs to be not only recognized but also highlighted. Locations, places, events, and activities that make expression of *multiple interests* possible by happenstance rather than by planning have proven especially important sources of learning opportunities. Children's festivals, neighborhood and nature trail walks, playgrounds, animal farms and petting zoos, fish ponds and hatcheries, and aviaries, to mention just a few, provide all kinds of opportunities to explore and learn.

A parent of two preschoolers, one with a disability, recently shared with us all the things that happened on a nature trail walk that became the foundation for learning. Picking flowers, collecting leaves, dropping stones in a creek, feeding birds bread crumbs, rolling around in the grass, chasing butterflies, and talking about a rabbit that happened by were just some of the things the children got to do while on their walk.

New experiences, even when they match children's interests, sometimes evoke unexpected responses (e.g., a child who likes being around other children becoming shy when taken to some type of group activity). A lesson learned from these experiences is not to give up too quickly. Persistence often pays off.

A two-year-old child with autism who liked playing soccer "froze" when he first attended a toddler soccer camp. The mother noticed that although her son wouldn't join the other children, he intently watched the other boys and girls kicking the soccer balls. The mother took her son back three more times before he felt comfortable getting on the field with the other children. Soccer became one of the boy's favorite things to do, and he became a star player as he grew older. As he approached his sixth birthday, the coaches were choosing players for different teams. Every coach wanted this boy on the team. The mother commented that this made her feel especially good about her decision (several years back) to pursue this activity for her son. She also said that this was the first time anyone had paid so much attention to her son because of what he could do rather than what he could not do.

Summary

Strategies have been provided for identifying children's interests and using them as a basis for promoting participation in community-based learning activities. Together with the methods described in Dunst et al. (in press), these strategies provide parents and practitioners several different ways of supporting and strengthening existing and emerging child abilities.

These methods and procedures address Urschel's (1998) challenge that children's full participation in community life should occur in ways that communicate ability rather than disability, commonalities rather than differences. Effective strategies are needed for children with disabilities and delays to realize their capabilities, and for community members to fully include these children and their families in all aspects of society. Interest-based participation in community activities is one such strategy.

Note

The methods and strategies described in this paper were supported, in part, by grants from the U.S. Department of Education, Office of Special Education Programs (HO24B60119, HO24B40020). Correspondence should be sent to Carl J. Dunst, Orelena Hawks Puckett Institute, 18A Regent Park Blvd., Asheville, NC 28806, or dunst@puckett.org.

References

Beckman, P., Barnwell, D., Horn, E., Hanson, M., Guitierrez, S., & Lieber, J. (1998). Communities, families and inclusion. *Early Childhood Research Quarterly, 13,* 125-150.

Bronfenbrenner, U. (1992). Ecological systems theory. In R. Vasta (Ed.), *Six theories of child development: Revised formulations and current issues* (pp. 187-248). Philadelphia: Jessica Kingsley.

Chen J.Q., Krechevsky, M., Viens, J., & Isberg, E. (1998). *Project Zero frameworks for early childhood education: Vol. 1 Building on children's strengths: The experience of Project Spectrum.* (H. Gardner, D.H. Feldman, & M. Krechevsky, Series Ed.). New York: Teachers College Press.

Dunst, C.J. (2000). Everyday children's learning opportunities: Characteristics and consequences. *Children's Learning Opportunities Report,* Vol. 2, No. 1.

Dunst, C.J. (in press). Participation of young children with disabilities in community learning activities. In M. Guralnick (Ed.), *Early childhood inclusion: Focus on change.* Baltimore: Paul H. Brookes.

Dunst, C.J. & Bruder, M.B. (1999). Family and community activity settings, natural learning environments, and children's learning opportunities. *Children's Learning Opportunities Report,* Vol. 1, No. 2.

Dunst, C.J., Bruder, M.B., Trivette, C.M., Raab, M., & McLean, M. (1998, May). *Increasing children's learning opportunities through families and communities; early childhood research institute: Year 2 progress report.* Asheville, NC: Orelena Hawks Puckett Institute.

Dunst, C.J. & Hamby, D. (1999). Family life as sources of children's learning opportunities. *Children's Learning Opportunities Report,* Vol. 1, No. 3.

Dunst, C.J., Hamby, D., Trivette, C.M., Raab, M., & Bruder, M.B. (2000). *Young children's participation in everyday family and community activity.* Manuscript submitted for publication.

Dunst, C.J., Herter, S., Shields, H., & Bennis, L. (in press). Mapping community-based natural learning opportunities. *Young Exceptional Children.*

Farver, J.A.M. (1999). Activity setting analysis: A model for examining the role of culture in development. In A. Göncü (Ed.), *Children's engagement in the world: Sociocultural perspectives* (pp. 99-127). Cambridge, England: Cambridge University Press.

Field, T. (1978). The three R's of infant-adult interactions: Rhythms, repertoires, and responsivity. *Journal of Pediatric Psychology, 3,* 131-136.

Fogel, A. (1997). Information, creativity, and culture. In C. Dent-Read & P. Zukow-Goldring (Eds.), *Evolving explanations of development: Ecological approaches to organism—environment systems* (pp. 413-443). Washington, DC: American Psychological Association.

Gauvain, M. (1999). Everyday opportunities for the development of planning skills: Sociocultural and family influences. In A. Göncü (Ed.), *Children's engagement in the world: Sociocultural perspectives* (pp. 173-201). Cambridge, England: Cambridge University Press.

Gelman, R., Massey, C.M., & McManus, M. (1991). Characterizing supporting environments for cognitive development: Lessons from children in a museum. In L.B. Resnick & J.M. Levine (Eds.), *Perspectives on socially shared cognition* (pp. 226-256). Washington, DC: American Psychological Association.

Göncü, A., Tuermer, U., Jain, J., & Johnson, D. (1999). Children's play as cultural activity. In A. Göncü (Ed.), *Children's engagement in the world: Sociocultural perspectives* (pp. 148-170). Cambridge, England: Cambridge University Press.

Guberman, S.R. (1999). Supportive environments for cognitive development: Illustrations from children's mathematical activities outside of school. In A. Göncü (Ed.), *Children's engagement in the world: Sociocultural perspectives* (pp. 202-227). Cambridge, England: Cambridge University Press.

Krechevsky, M. (1998). *Project Zero frameworks for early childhood education: Vol. 3. Project Spectrum: Preschool assessment handbook.* (H. Gardner, D.H. Feldman, & M. Krechevsky, Series Ed.). New York: Teachers College Press.

LeeKeenan D. & Nimmo, J. (1993). Connections: Using the project approach with 2- and 3-year-olds in a university laboratory school. In C. Edwards, L. Gandini, & G. Forman (Eds.), *The hundred languages of children: The Reggio Emilia approach to early childhood education* (pp. 251-267). Norwood, NJ: Ablex.

MacTurk, R.H. & Morgan, G.A. (Eds.). (1995). *Advances in applied developmental psychology: Vol. 12. Mastery motivation: Origins, conceptualizations, and applications.* Norwood, NJ: Ablex.

Mandler, J.M. (2000). Perceptual and conceptual processes in infancy. *Journal of Cognition and Development, 1,* 3-36.

McWilliam, R.A. & Ware, W.B. (1994). The reliability of observations of young children's engagement: An application of generalizability theory. *Journal of Early Intervention, 18,* 34-47.

Moss, J. (1997). *The child preference indicators.* Unpublished paper, University Affiliated Program of Oklahoma, College of Medicine, University of Oklahoma Health Services Center, Oklahoma City. (Publication No. CA597.jm).

Nelson, K. (1999, Winter). Making sense: Language and thought in development. *Developmental Psychologist,* 1-10.

Rogoff, B., Mistry, J., Göncü, A., & Mosier, C. (1993). Guided participation in cultural activities by toddlers and caregivers. *Monographs of the Society for Research in Child Development, 58*(8, Serial No. 236).

Umstead, S., Boyd, K., & Dunst, C.J. (1995). Building community resources: Enabling inclusion in community programs and activities. *Exceptional Parent*, *25*(7), 36-37.

Urschel, K. (1998). Connecting with communities: Kids need kids. In L. Meyer, H. Park, M. Grenot-Scheyer, I. Schwartz, & B. Harry (Eds.), *Making friends: The influence of culture and development* (pp. 369-374). Baltimore: Paul H. Brookes.

Wolery, M. & Sainato, D.M. (1996). General curriculum and intervention strategies. In S.L. Odom & M.E. McLean (Eds.), *Early intervention/early childhood special education: Recommended practices* (pp. 125-158). Austin, TX: PRO-ED.

The Visiting Teacher

A Model of Inclusive ECSE Service Delivery

Eva Horn, Ph.D., University of Kansas
Susan Sandall, Ph.D., University of Washington

Pam completes a quick mental check of her planner page for the day. First there is Hillsboro Center at 8:30 A.M. where she needs to check in with Mindy's educational assistant on how the toilet training is coming along and collect data on Sam's use of descriptive labels. Then it's on to Town Centre to observe Kenny during large motor time to help generate some ideas for supporting him in initiating and sustaining appropriate interactions with his peers. She's got the copy of the peer affection games article that she promised to bring Kenny's teacher, Ms. Jane. Then it's on to Rockland Head Start to meet the physical therapist to put together plans for when and how Jenny can use the pronestander and improve the sitting support for Susie during snack. Next comes Woodlawn Preschool for a naptime meeting where the priority agenda item is strategies for getting Joey to pay attention during circle time. Pam checks that she has her notes on the video clip she made last week. At the last minute she decides to drop in her copy of the tape just as a backup in case the preschool teacher forgets hers. Finally, she checks that she has her materials together for the afternoon orientation visit with Juan, his mother, and the Spanish interpreter to the center where Juan will begin attending next week.

The provision of early childhood special education (ECSE) is changing. Inclusion of young children with disabilities in settings with typically developing children is occurring with increasing frequency in school systems and communities (Wolery et al., 1993). The requirement in PL 99-457, that all states provide public education for three- to five-year-old children with disabilities beginning in the 1991/92 school year resulted in increased pressure on many local school systems to find age appropriate early education settings (Rose & Smith, 1994). Most public school systems do not have readily available, typical preschool settings because they do not regularly provide services to three- and four-year-old children without disabilities. Even those systems that may provide some preschool services (e.g., Head Start, low income, and at-risk early education programs) frequently have separate administrative structures and service standards for these and the special education program. Therefore, an array of strategies or models have been developed in response, including bringing typical children into ECSE settings (reverse mainstreaming); pairing two separate classrooms together for part of the day (buddy classroom); mingling funds, programs, and personnel in one classroom (team teaching); placing children in typical preschool setting (e.g., community child care, publicly funded preschool programs); and providing ECSE services through a visiting teacher (ECSE itinerant teaching model). For more extensive descriptions of service delivery models and the organizational contexts in which they occur see Odom and colleagues (1999) report based on their in-depth study of 16 inclusive programs across the United States.

The last approach identified above, and the one in which Pam is engaged, the itinerant teaching model, is becoming more prevalent (Brown et al., 1996; Bruder, 1998; Bruder, 1993; Bruder, Sachs, & Deiner, 1990; Hanline, 1990; Templeman, Fredricks, & Udell, 1989). While more examples and demonstrations are being provided in the literature, little information is available on specific strategies for effectively implementing the model. That is, what does it look like on a day-to-day basis? How are the roles for the ECSE itinerant defined and developed such that children are provided flexible levels and types of support to ensure their continued participation and active development? This article provides descriptions of the primary components of the ECSE itinerant teacher's roles and responsibilities, as well as specific strategies for facilitating success in implementing the model. The primary sources of information for these descriptions are two large urban school systems both implementing an ECSE itinerant service approach. Extended involvement with these two school systems occurred over several years as part of an Office of Special Education Programs (OSEP) model demonstration project (i.e., Project BLEND, Horn, Heiser, Odom & Brown, 1998) and through the Early Childhood Research Institute on Inclusion (ECRII, 2000).

Defining Collaborative Consultation Itinerant Teaching

In itinerant teaching, services are provided on a regular basis in early childhood education settings by ECSE teachers and related service personnel (e.g., physical therapists, speech therapists, vision teacher).

Itinerant teachers and other related service personnel visit the settings rather than being housed there permanently. These specialized personnel work with the early childhood education lead teachers in the settings to systematically embed individualized educational goals for children in curriculum activities and classroom routines. The model has the following primary components of service: (1) participation in a typical preschool or child care with same age peers; (2) regular visits by an ECSE itinerant teacher to support the child's placement, and implementation and monitoring of the child's Individual Educational Program (IEP); (3) provision of eligible related services to the child in the setting; and (4) transportation to and from the setting. The approach is one of collaboration between early childhood educators, ECSE teachers and related services, and families to support the child's development as specified in the IEP and simultaneously allowing full participation and inclusion in typical settings.

A primary role of the itinerant ECSE teacher is collaborative consultation with the child care or preschool personnel. The purpose of collaboration is to enhance the participation of children in common preschool activities within their child care or preschool program. A fundamental aspect of collaborative consultation is the understanding that child care personnel and ECSE teachers are partners in determining the best methods of promoting children's active engagement within the context of the preschool or child care activities and settings. Goals for children's IEP are developed with active involvement of team members (e.g., early childhood teachers, families, ECSE itinerant teachers, related services) to insure the maximum feasibility of the individual plans within the context of children's preschool programs.

A primary mechanism for implementing the collaborative consultation process is regular visits to the preschool or child care setting. These visits are used to share information about the child's needs and progress, and possible activities and strategies that could promote children's active participation. After observing and participating with children in their programs, the itinerant teacher and the early childhood educator discuss how best to support and promote children's development during classroom routines and activities. At times the itinerant teacher provides supplemental information about facilitating young children's development by demonstrating effective procedures for promoting children's engagement in the classroom.

Roles and Responsibilities of the Itinerant Teacher

Both the above definition of the model and the opening vignette sharing a typical day for Pam (an ECSE itinerant teacher) illustrate the necessity for staff members to forge new relationships and assume new roles. The itinerant teacher's roles and responsibilities can be more clearly described by addressing two components: (1) managing collaboration with multiple partners; and (2) the content of the consultation. Each component will be described in more detail.

Managing Collaboration With Multiple Partners

The need for frequent communication, coordination, and cooperation, which nurture partnerships among the array of adults with whom itinerant teachers find themselves working, is fundamental to making the model work. The itinerant teacher, educational assistants, related services personnel, early childhood teacher and assistant teacher, family members and other support members (such as interpreters) involved with the child constitute the child's planning team. Parents and early childhood educators are crucial team members. They can provide indispensable information about the child as well as feedback regarding the feasibility of individual goals for children and their families. Because the early childhood educators most often implement the strategies used to meet goals, they are essential for determining whether or not particular strategies should be used given the resources and circumstance of the preschool classroom. Communication, both informal and formal, and coordination are key for working effectively as an ECSE itinerant teacher.

Communication. ECSE itinerant teachers must be skilled in relaying and receiving information from a variety of sources. In Pam's daily schedule, we see examples of a variety of communication partners (i.e., educational assistant, early childhood teacher, physical therapist, parent, and interpreter). Across the course of Pam's day, we also see her use multiple formats to both receive and relay information. These include: (1) structured data collection (i.e., Sam's descriptive labels); (2) semi-structured observation notes (i.e., Kenny's social initiations in large motor time); (3) written resource materials (i.e., affection games article, children's book on children with diverse abilities to be read to children in Juan's new center); (4) face-to-face interaction and demonstration (i.e., as the physical therapist and Pam work together with Jenny and Susie to address positioning issues); (5) group discussion based on videotaped sample; (6) co-visiting for immediate information exchange (i.e., both with the physical therapist and with Juan's mother); and (7) searching the World Wide Web for information on the new communication device recommended by the speech therapist for Jenny and posting a question to a listserv for information on how to adapt it for Jenny's specific situations. Each of the preceding examples provide general strategies that have been tailored to address the child and setting needs at the current point in time.

Itinerant ECSE teachers, such as Pam, also engage in a series of regular systematic communication procedures including "naptime visits," "visit notes," and "communication notebooks." As a direct response to concerns about when preschool teachers had time to plan, the concept of naptime visits evolved. These visits are held on a regular schedule once or twice a month typically during the young children's rest or naptime (hence the name) when the early childhood educator is better able to meet and plan collaboratively. Agendas for naptime meetings are very specific and require that necessary preparation and support information has been collected and disseminated ahead of time as was the case with Pam's scheduled naptime visit for addressing Joey's circle time behavior. Time is limited and must be used wisely. Naptime visits have proven invaluable for promoting communication and addressing any questions, concerns, or needs for additional information that team members have. In addition, all team members are invited to the naptime meetings, and at times arrangements are made to ensure that particular team members are present to provide their expertise on a specific agenda item.

Following all child care or preschool and naptime visits, the itinerant teacher writes visit notes. The notes are written on self-copying paper such that the itinerant teacher has a copy and one is placed in the child's communication notebook. Visit notes include a general summary of the events of the visit, responses to questions or concerns that have arisen since the previous visit, and notes about the child's progress. In addition, "to do items" are included for both the itinerant and the early childhood educator. These will aid them in preparing for the next visit. For example, Pam's visit note on Kenny the previous week would have included a note to bring along the peer affection games article. The communication notebook is used by all team members, including the family, to communicate relevant information. For example, the Rockland Head Start teacher may have noted that Susie was having problems with sliding out of her chair during snack time. Pam noted this at the beginning of one of her biweekly visits and also noted that the physical therapist had indicated that she would like to see Jenny using a pronestander. Pam communicated the need to meet together at the center to address these two concerns. Once this was scheduled it was added to the communication notebook. Jenny's mother read the note and made arrangements to be at the center so that she could see how the pronestander worked. Thus parents, preschool and itinerant teachers, and related service providers can all use communication notebooks to facilitate frequent and clear communication among team members.

Coordinating Input. Again, looking over the tasks on Pam's daily planner we can see the critical role of coordinator of information exchange on the itinerant teacher's success. As one related service provider noted, "I see Pam (the itinerant teacher) as the orchestra conductor and the rest of us play supporting roles. The preschool teacher carries the main melody line and the rest of us are to come in and harmonize as needed and on our scheduled basis."

Adults working and playing well together for the child's benefit depends on the development of positive relationships based on mutual respect. Children with disabilities need the expertise of many professionals and significant adults in their lives. As an itinerant teacher stated, "None of us has any magic that we bring to the situation; together we can make it work."

Major Areas of Consultation Content

The itinerant teachers need to create and coordinate resources and plans that support the inclusion of young children with disabilities. Following are content areas that itinerant teachers need to address as they relay and receive information related to supporting children's active participation and development in inclusive settings.

Physical Access and Accommodations. The itinerant teacher, through observation and discussion with other team members, needs to ensure that the physical arrangement of the classroom is such that all areas and materials are accessible to all children, including those with physical or sensory limitations (Hanline, 1993). For example, a child with fine motor limitations may have difficulty turning the pages of a book. Turning the pages can be simplified by gluing a small piece of foam to each page, which will separate them. Pam is having the physical therapist help develop an adaptation to provide Susie with more stability while sitting at the classroom table during snack. The therapist suggests that she needs flexion in her hips to reduce her tone and needs to keep her hips firmly in the back of the chair. Together they use cardboard blocks to build up the foot position and place bath appliques on the back of the chair seat to accomplish this. On another day Pam notices that as Susie works to scoop the pudding for snack with her spoon the bowl slides away from her. Pam places a non-slip mat under the bowl.

Sometimes accommodations require the itinerant teacher to pull in a resource person, while at other times the accommodations are more readily apparent. In the case of Jenny's accommodations, the physical therapist, speech therapist, and assistive technology specialist needed to be involved. Likewise, accommodations for Juan's family to fully understand the new program's approach and philosophy required a bilingual interpreter.

Accommodations and Supports for Social Inclusion. One of the most important aspects of successful inclusion for young children with disabilities is social inclusion (Odom & McEvoy, 1990). However, social interactions between children with and without disabilities frequently do not occur spontaneously (Guralnick, 1990). The itinerant teacher can help the classroom teacher implement general classroom strategies known to facilitate child-to-child interactions (Odom & Brown, 1993). Social interaction occurs more often during less structured activities such as free play. Certain toys and materials such as dress-up, housekeeping, cars and trucks, and block play are more conducive to social interactions. Teachers can also provide support for social interactions by observing and giving positive feedback to the children involved. To enhance the likelihood that children with disabilities will have positive social interactions, the teacher could arrange groups so that children who are socially skilled are included with children whose disabilities have interfered with social development. Sometimes the itinerant might provide the teacher with specific strategies designed to teach a child with disabilities behaviors for initiating and maintaining social interactions. Kenny's teachers, Pam and Ms. Jane, have determined this is an issue for him and are in the process of developing and implementing an intervention plan. An initial step planned is to have the teacher verbally guide him and model how to enter into an ongoing group game during the gym time freeplay. In addition, she will be available to assist the peers in interpreting his request and making a place for him in the

activity. Ms. Jane will e-mail Pam at the end of the week about the success of the strategies she is trying with Kenny.

Accommodations and Supports for Active Engagement in Activities. Active engagement with materials and activities is central to a child's learning and positive development (Dunst, McWilliams, & Holbert, 1986). In accordance with developmentally appropriate practice guidelines, the early childhood curriculum should emphasize play, discovery, and problem solving for skill mastery and fostering independence. Sometimes children with disabilities need additional supports in order to remain actively engaged (Lieber, Schwartz, Sandall, Horn, & Wolery, 1999). The itinerant teacher can assist the preschool teacher in identifying the contexts in which the child may become inattentive. Together they can then establish strategies for increasing the child's length of attending and the complexity of his/her engagement. Pam and the teachers at Woodlawn Preschool are going to use a video clip of Joey in circle time to develop a workable plan for understanding and supporting Joey's active participation.

Identification and Implementation of Child's Goals and Objectives. Early childhood special education emphasizes the importance of intervention to prevent or reduce the effect of a disability on children's development (Carta, Schwartz, Atwater, & McConnell, 1991). Emphasis is on providing a range of services and individualized teaching plans. The itinerant teacher must identify how the child's specific goals and objectives can be included in each classroom activity. For example, a routine classroom activity such as snack time would provide an opportunity to work on eating independently (adaptive behavior goal), picking up small bite size foods (fine motor), and requesting additional snack items (language). Supporting the goals and objectives of related service providers in feasible and meaningful ways within classroom activities is also necessary. Pam will work with the Head Start teacher to determine appropriate times and contexts during which Jenny can be positioned in the pronestander to work on lower extremity weight bearing. For Juan, she will visit the new center with him, his mother, and the interpreter to facilitate the transition to the new program and communicate his individualized goals and objectives as a first step in planning for their embedding into the new setting.

Monitoring and Modifications to Address Changes in Support. Systematic, regular evaluation of the child's progress in attaining individual goals and objectives is a critical component of ECSE (Carta et al., 1991). These evaluations not only provide clear and direct methods for communicating the growth and development of the child, but are extremely useful in promoting timely decision making related to changes in intervention strategies to maximize the child's learning. Pam's data collection system for Sam's use of descriptive labels actually has two purposes. First, she wants to ensure that Sam is provided with a sufficient number of opportunities to practice language. Second, she will use the information for reporting his progress as a part of his IEP.

Conclusion

The description of Pam's preparation for her day at the beginning of this article provides a glimpse of the range of roles and responsibilities that are the day-to-day work of an ECSE itinerant teacher. Ultimately the successful fulfillment of the role requires an acceptance of diversity, a commitment to the rights of all children to be educated with their peers, a willingness to work collaboratively in partnership with others on behalf of children, and the ability to be innovative and flexible. As one itinerant stated in describing what she does, "I do a little bit of every-thing. ... I'm a teacher, I'm a pair of hands, I pass out milk. ... each center is different; I just have to find my way with each center."

Note

Preparation of this manuscript was supported by the Early Education Program for Children with Disabilities of the U.S. Department of Education (i.e., Model Demonstration Projects—Grant # H024B10108 and the Early Childhood Research Institute on Inclusion—Grant # H023A30035). Address correspondence to Eva M. Horn, Dept. of Special Education, 521 JR Pearson, University of Kansas, Lawrence, KS 66045, E-mail:evahorn@ukans.edu

References

Brown, W.H., Horn, E.M., Heiser, J.G., & Odom, S.L. (1996). Project BLEND: An inclusive model of early intervention services. *Journal of Early Intervention, 20*(4), 364-375.

Bruder, M.B. (1998). A collaborative model to increase the capacity of childcare providers to include young children with disabilities. *Journal of Early Intervention, 21*(2), 177-186.

Bruder, M.B., (1993). The provision of early intervention and early childhood special education within community early childhood programs: Characteristics of effective service delivery. *Topics in Early Childhood Special Education, 13*(1), 19-37.

Bruder, M.B., Sachs, S., & Deiner, P. (1990). Models of integration through early intervention/childcare collaboration. *Zero to Three, 10*(3), 14-17.

Carta, J., Schwartz, I., Atwater, J., & McConnell, S. (1991). Developmentally appropriate practice: Appraising its usefulness for young children with disabilities. *Topics in Early Childhood Special Education, 11*(1), 1-20.

Dunst, C.J., McWilliams, R.A., & Holbert, K. (1986). Assessment of preschool classroom environments. *Diagnostique, 11,* 212-232.

ECRII (Early Childhood Research Institute on Inclusion) Researchers (2000). *ECRII final report.* Washington, DC: Research Institute Funded by U.S. Department of Education.

Guralnick, M. (1990). Social competence and early intervention. *Journal of Early Intervention, 14,* 3-14.

Hanline, M.F. (1993). Inclusion of preschoolers with profound disabilities: An analysis of children's inter-actions. *Journal of the Association for Persons with Severe Handicaps, 18*(1), 28-35.

Hanline, M. (1990). Project profiles: A consulting model for providing integration opportunities for pre-school children with disabilities. *Journal of Early Intervention, 14*(4), 360-366.

Horn, E.M., Heiser, J.G., Odom, S.L., & Brown, W.H. (1998). *Project BLEND (Beginning Learning Experiences in Developmentally Inclusive Childcare and at Home): Final report.* Washington, DC: Model Demonstration Project Funded by U.S. Department of Education.

Lieber, J., Schwartz, I., Sandall, S., Horn, E., & Wolery, R. (1999). Curricular considerations for young children in inclusive settings. In C. Seifert (Ed.), *The early childhood curriculum: Current findings in theory and practice* (pp. 243-264). New York: Teachers College Press.

Odom, S. & Brown, W. (1993). Social interaction skills intervention for young children with disabilities in integrated settings. In C.A. Peck, S.L. Odom, & D.D. Bricker (Eds.), *Integrating young children with disabilities into community programs* (pp. 39-64). Baltimore: Paul H. Brookes.

Odom, S., Horn, E., Marquart, J., Hanson, M., Wolfberg, P., Beckman, P., Lieber, J., Li, S., Schwartz, I., Janko, S., & Sandall, S. (1999). On the forms of inclusion: Organizational context and individualized service models. *Journal of Early Intervention, 22*(3), 185-199.

Odom, S. & McEvoy, M. (1990). Mainstreaming at the preschool level: Potential barriers and tasks for the field. *Topics in Early Childhood Special Education, 10*(2), 48-61.

Rose, D. & Smith, B. (1994). Providing public education services to preschoolers with disabilities in community programs: Who's responsible for what? *Young Children, 49*(6), 64-68.

Templeman, T.P., Fredricks, H.D., & Udell, T. (1989). Integration of children with moderate and severe handicaps into day care centers. *Journal of Early Intervention, 12*(4), 315-328.

Wolery, M., Holcombe, A., Venn, M.L., Brookfield, J., Huffman, K., Schroeder, C., Martin, C.G., & Fleming, L.A. (1993). Mainstreaming in early childhood programs: Current status and relevant issues. *Young Children, 49*(1), 78-84.

The Other Children at Preschool

Experiences of Typically Developing Children in Inclusive Programs

Karen E. Diamond, Ph.D., Purdue University
Susan Stacey, B.A., Purdue University

According to recent Census Bureau figures, more than 4 million three- and four-year-old children attend a preschool program for at least part of the day (U.S. Census Bureau, 1998). Estimates of the proportions of preschool programs that enroll at least one child with a disability range from 34% of child care programs (Buysse, Wesley, Bryant, & Gardner, 1999) to 74% of early childhood programs (Wolery et al., 1993). Even if we take the more conservative estimate (that 1/3 of early childhood programs are inclusive ones), more than 1.5 million preschool children are attending school with one or more classmates who have identified disabilities.

Why is it important that we pay attention to the experiences of typically developing children in inclusive programs? Inclusion is a life-long process that has the goal of full participation for children and adults within education, community activities, and work (Kliewer, 1999). Twenty years after they leave preschool, typically developing children (now adults!) will be members of communities that include adults with disabilities. There is ample evidence that attitudes toward others are learned, and that the development of attitudes begins during the preschool years (Ramsey & Myers, 1990). If children's experiences in inclusive preschool programs are positive ones, these experiences support the development of positive attitudes toward people with disabilities. Similarly, negative experiences in inclusive preschool settings may be precursors to later, more rigid, prejudices about people with disabilities (Stoneman, 1993). For people with disabilities, negative attitudes may be just as effective as physical, architectural barriers in limiting opportunities to participate fully in schools, jobs, and communities. Prior experience, it seems, may have an effect on typically developing children's subsequent responses to classmates with disabilities. In this article, we examine research on the development of children's ideas about people with disabilities. The examples in this article come from our observations at Purdue University's Child Development Laboratory School which offers inclusive programs for three-, four-, and five-year-old children.

Greg and Brittany are typically developing four-year olds. One of their classmates, Tara, has significantly delayed motor and language skills. Greg appears fascinated by Tara's wheelchair; he often stands nearby and watches intently as a teacher helps Tara to participate in classroom activities. Brittany, on the other hand, is very matter-of-fact about Tara's disability. Her older brother had severe multiple disabilities, and she is used to being with children who cannot walk or talk. Sometimes Brittany offers to help so that Tara can participate in an activity.

Children's Understanding of Disabilities

What is it like for typically developing children to have a classmate with a disability? Research has demonstrated that preschool children know quite a lot about physical and sensory disabilities, particularly when a child uses adaptive equipment, regardless of children's experiences with people with these disabilities. For instance, we found that most three-

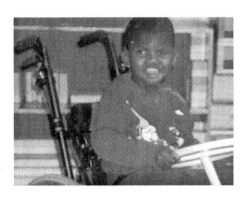

and four-year olds thought that someone who used a wheelchair or was blind would have trouble walking, and that someone who wore a hearing aid would have trouble hearing. Children held these ideas even if they had never been in a class with a child with a disability. Having equipment that they can see seems to make it easier for children to understand a disability (Diamond, Hestenes, Carpenter, & Innes, 1997). Adaptive equipment can also be confusing. When we talked with one five-year old about what it might be like to be deaf, he suggested that someone who is deaf "can't hear because he has those things [hearing aids] in his ears. He could hear if he took them out." (Diamond & Hestenes, 1994). Having classmates with special needs promotes typically developing children's appreciation for the capabilities of each classmate.

Now that they've been together for several months, the kids know that Tara has a sense of humor and will tease; they know Robin can read anything (and sometimes look to her if they are stumped); and they know that Brian is the most helpful child in class when it comes to finding lost shoes and socks.

Mental retardation and emotional disturbance are disabilities that are more difficult for children to understand. We have found that when preschool children look at photographs, they do not appear to notice the facial characteristics that are unique to children with Down syndrome (Diamond & Hestenes, 1996; Innes & Diamond, 1999). This is in contrast to older children who rely on facial characteristics to identify others as "retarded" or "not retarded" (Goodman, 1989). Thus, unlike older children, preschoolers may be initially unaware of the disabilities of some of their classmates, particularly if the classmate uses no specialized equipment. In fact, research suggests that young children are not even aware of the possibility that someone might have a disability that is related to difficulties in thinking, such as mental retardation or emotional disturbance (Conant & Budoff, 1983; Diamond & Hestenes, 1996).

Even young children develop a more complex understanding of disabilities when they attend an inclusive program. We found, for example, that preschool children who had a classmate who was deaf had a much better understanding of sign language, and of the connection between hearing and talking, than did children without this experience. In addition, children developed a better understanding that disabilities do not disappear—that a child with cerebral palsy is likely to have a disability as an adult—when they had classmates with disabilities.

In the Lab School, the children are careful observers of the therapists and paraprofessionals. They know that Beth comes to school to help Tara with a walker, and that Kristin teaches Robin new ways of talking. One day, Jung-Min noticed Karen teaching Robin a phrase for getting what she wanted at the water table ("I want a blue fish, please"). When Robin reached for Jung-Min's fish, she held it away from Robin and waited for her to use the phrase, which she did. Jung-Min handed her the fish, and beamed .... she knew Robin had learned something appropriate and seemed to feel that she had contributed to this.

Young children use knowledge that they already possess (for example, that you can be hurt in an accident or that babies do not talk) to explain something they are only beginning to understand (a child's disability). Children often attributed a classmate's braces, walker, or wheelchair to an accident in which "he broke his leg," or explained a peer's difficulty talking by saying, "he can't talk because he's a baby; when he gets older, he'll be able to talk just like me." In addition, children often focus on one or two important features (such as equipment or significantly delayed skills) in determining whether or not a child has a disability. Children may use this awareness to judge how similar or dissimilar a child with a disability is to him/herself.

Children's Acceptance of Others

What do children learn from experiences in inclusive preschools? According to parents, preschool children become more accepting of human differences, more aware of the needs of others, show less discomfort with people with disabilities, are less prejudiced, have fewer stereotypes about people who are different, and are more responsive and helpful to other children after their enrollment in an inclusive program (Peck, Carlson, & Helmstetter, 1992). When we asked children about how they might solve a series of hypothetical classroom dilemmas that included a child with a disability, we found that children in inclusive classes had significantly more ideas about how they might be helpful, and were significantly more likely to refer to a child's disability, than were children in classes with only typically developing classmates (Diamond & Carpenter, 2000). These qualities are evident in our observations of children's interactions in the spring of the school year.

The children no longer pay much attention to all the adaptive equipment Tara uses, and will sometimes go get it for her, or go with her to get her other chair. Just the other day, Greg commented that Tara liked to play with tools and "fix" things. He spontaneously got a screwdriver and "fixed" her wheelchair.

Brittany laid down on the floor and began doing exercises while the physical therapist was doing stretches with Tara. Once Brittany started this, several other children joined in. Another child, recognizing that Tara hates doing stretches, sometimes brings her a book to look at, or gets the tape recorder so she can listen to music.

Children's Interactions

Research has consistently demonstrated that children with disabilities are included less often in interactive play activities than are their typically developing peers. Although the degree of social separation between peers with and without disabilities appears to vary with the severity of the child's delays, even children with mild delays are less accepted as playmates than are their typically developing classmates (Guralnick, Connor, Hammond, Gottman, & Kinnish, 1996). In an observational study, Brown and his colleagues found that typically developing children were significantly more likely to direct interactions toward typically developing classmates than toward classmates with disabilities (Brown, Odom, Li, & Zercher, 1999). Despite this, children with disabilities interacted frequently with their typically developing peers in both of these studies.

If the idea of "playing together" is expanded to include parallel play activities in addition to more complex social interactions, several research studies have demonstrated that children with disabilities are often included in activities that involve peers without disabilities. Okagaki and her colleagues found that children with disabilities participated in activities with their typically developing classmates as often as did peers without disabilities (Okagaki, Diamond, Kontos, & Hestenes, 1998). These results are similar to those of Brown and his colleagues (1999) who found that children with disabilities participated in social groups with at least one classmate without a disability during 73% of the intervals that they observed. Taken together, these results suggest that children with disabilities are included in common events in preschool classrooms, although their level of social participation tends to be less than for typically developing children.

The children play alongside Robin even if they themselves are capable of cooperative play. They seem to realize that she is not. For instance, Robin loves Marbleworks. One day, Sara approached her very quietly, didn't speak or ask for anything, picked up an occasional marble and rolled it down, waiting for Robin to look

*and take a turn. In this way, they were able to take turns, unusual
for Robin.*

Teachers and Parents as Models

We know little about the ways in which teachers' behaviors affect the
development of children's ideas about, and attitudes toward, people
with disabilities. Research suggests, however, that when children are
divided into groups based on whether or not they have a disability, this
may encourage typically developing children to think about their classmates with disabilities as different from themselves (e.g., Bigler, Jones,
& Lobliner, 1997). For example, Schnorr (1990) studied typically developing first-graders' perceptions of Peter, a child with Down syndrome

who was included in their class for part of
each school day. While teachers and parents thought that this part-time inclusion
was quite successful, these first-graders
thought that Peter was different from
themselves. They attributed his 'difference' to factors that separated him from
his classmates: he left the classroom for
specialized services, did different work,
and rode a different bus. More recently,
Janko and her colleagues (Janko,
Schwartz, Sandall, Anderson & Cottam,
1997) identified a number of practices in
inclusive preschool programs that separated children with disabilities from their
classmates. In one school district, children with disabilities were transported to
school by a district school bus, while children without disabilities were transported by their families (a common
practice in many programs). Children
questioned "the difference between the 'car kids' and the 'bus kids'" (p.
293) who not only rode a bus but also stayed at school for lunch. For
these children, whether or not you rode a bus was an important char-
acteristic that divided them into children with disabilities (bus kids) and
children without disabilities (car kids). Conversely, in another child care
classroom, each child had an assigned chair, not just the child with
Down syndrome whose chair had been modified by the physical

therapist. By using this strategy, teachers met one child's need for a chair that provided more support without marking that child as different from the rest of the group. Similarly, integrated rather than pull-out therapies that allow children with disabilities to remain part of the classroom group may facilitate children's views of their classmates with disabilities as important members of their class (Diamond & Cooper, 2000; McWilliam, 1996). To the extent that classroom experiences promote more opportunities for all children to work and play together, and fewer opportunities for children with disabilities to be seen as members of an "out-group" who are "not like me," such experiences may also promote the development of more positive attitudes toward classmates with disabilities. This is evident in the following comment from Robin's teacher.

Sometimes we'll try to point out a particular skill. For instance, Robin is the only child in her class who knows how to read. At Large Group, when children are learning to read their names and the names of their classmates, if someone is stuck, we'll say "I wonder if Robin knows?" She will usually read it for the child. If we can find more things that she can do ... then I think they might see her as a capable person who understands what is going on.

Parents of children with disabilities play an important role in promoting children's understanding of their child (Turnbull, Pereira, & Blue-Banning, 1999). One strategy that has been used by parents of children with disabilities in our inclusive program is to provide other parents with specific information about their child's disability. This serves many purposes: it gives the parents of a child with a disability an opportunity to talk about their child with other parents; it helps to answer other parents' unasked questions about a child's disability; and it gives parents the information they may need when responding to their child's questions. In addition to communicating with other parents, parents of children with disabilities often have opportunities to talk about their child's disability with his or her classmates (Turnbull & Turnbull, 1991). Sometimes this is done while explaining about special equipment. Recently, one of the parents in our program talked with her daughter's classmates about having a child with a disability.

Brittany, a typically developing four-year old, had a brother with a disability who died last year. She often talks about her brother—matter of factly, but expressing sadness. Her words and her comfort level tell us that she has discussed this often, and has thought about it a great deal. During Special Family Week (a sharing time when families come in and do activities or speak with all the children about the child's family), Brittany's mother came to visit. She brought along Brittany's year-old brother, and told the children gently and frankly that "... actually Brittany has two brothers. Her older brother, Mark, was very sick when he was born. He could not walk or eat (here Brittany intercedes to tell the children that he 'was fed through a tube in his belly button') and died when he was five years old. We all miss him a lot and think of him every day. We are sad sometimes, but we remember that he was very happy when he was with us, and we have things to remember him by." At this point, Brittany took a photograph of her brother around for all the children to see. The other children looked and listened very intently to this. No children referred to this again in class, but several parents mentioned that their child had told Brittany's story at home, not because they were disturbed by it, but because they understood—to some extent—what had happened, and wanted to share what they knew. Parents were impressed by their acceptance of the facts, as were we.

Discussions between children and parents about classmates with disabilities are likely to be common. The ways in which parents respond to children's questions are important in promoting children's acceptance of their classmates (Okagaki et al., 1998).

Suggestions for Practice

There is evidence that the structure of the classroom may influence children's ideas about their peers with disabilities (Schnorr, 1990). The following suggestions for practice reflect results from research and are ones that we have implemented in our program.

- Work with specialists so that therapies are provided within the classroom.
- Encourage therapists to include typically developing children in the therapy session.
- Encourage children's interests in adaptive equipment and develop ways that they explore and help set up equipment.
- Ensure that children sit together *in similar seating* for social events such as snack, lunch, or group time. In our program, therapists have developed a variety of adapted seating arrangements so that children who need additional support are able to sit with their peers for group events.
- Find out what each child can do and emphasize this with other children.

- Draw attention to positive personality traits that are shared among all children.
- Assign "buddies" for some activities so that all children have an opportunity to play with each of their classmates.
- Take advantage of children's shared interests and prompt interactions between classmates.

Research suggests that typically developing children's attitudes toward people with disabilities will be closely associated with children's awareness of disability, the ways in which teachers and parents foster the inclusion of children with disabilities in school and community settings, and the quality and extent of children's interactions with classmates with disabilities during the early school years. When children accept the responsibility for ensuring that a classmate with a disability is included in classroom activities (Salisbury & Palombaro, 1998), wait for a classmate in a wheelchair to "catch up" with the group (Janney & Snell, 1996), or offer assistance to a classmate (Richardson & Schwartz, 1998), these behaviors tell us that children are both aware of a child's disability-related limitations and think of that child as part of their peer group.

References

Bigler, R.S., Jones, L.C., & Lobliner, D.B. (1997). Social categorization and the formation of intergroup attitudes in children. *Child Development, 68*, 530-543.

Brown, W.H., Odom, S.L., Li, S., & Zercher, C. (1999). Ecobehavioral assessment in early childhood programs: A portrait of preschool inclusion. *The Journal of Special Education, 33*, 138-153.

Buysse, V., Wesley, P.W., Bryant, D., & Gardner, D. (1999). Quality of early childhood programs in inclusive and noninclusive settings. *Exceptional Children, 65*, 301-314.

Conant, S. & Budoff, M. (1983). Patterns of awareness in children's understanding of disability. *Mental Retardation, 21*, 119-125.

Diamond, K.E. & Carpenter, C. (2000). The influence of inclusive preschool programs on children's sensitivity to the needs of others. *Journal of Early Intervention, 23*, 81-91.

Diamond, K.E. & Cooper, D. (2000). Children's perspectives on the roles of teachers and therapists in inclusive early childhood programs. *Early Education and Development, 11*, 203-216.

Diamond, K.E. & Hestenes, L. (1994). Preschool children's understanding of disability: Experiences leading to the elaboration of the concept of hearing loss. *Early Education and Development, 5*, 301-309.

Diamond, K.E. & Hestenes, L. (1996). Preschool children's conceptions of disabilities: The salience of disability in children's ideas about others. *Topics in Early Childhood Special Education, 16*, 458-475.

Diamond, K.E., Hestenes, L., Carpenter, E., & Innes, F. (1997). Relationships between enrollment in an inclusive class and preschool children's ideas about people with disabilities. *Topics in Early Childhood Special Education, 17*, 520-536.

Goodman, J. (1989). Does retardation mean dumb? Children's perceptions of the nature, cause, and course of mental retardation. *The Journal of Special Education, 23*, 313-329.

Guralnick, M.J., Connor, R., Hammond, M., Gottman, J.M., & Kinnish, K. (1996). Immediate effects of mainstreamed settings on the social interactions and social integration of preschool children. *American Journal on Mental Retardation, 100*, 359-378.

Innes, F. & Diamond, K.E. (1999). Typically developing children's interactions with peers with disabilities: Relationships between mothers' comments and children's ideas about disabilities. *Topics in Early Childhood Special Education, 19*, 103-111.

Janko, S., Schwartz, I., Sandall, S., Anderson, K., & Cottam, C. (1997). Beyond microsystems: Unanticipated lessons about the meaning of inclusion. *Topics in Early Childhood Special Education, 17*, 286-306.

Janney, R.E. & Snell, M.E. (1996). How teachers use peer interactions to include students with moderate and severe disabilities in elementary general education classrooms. *Journal of the Association for Persons with Severe Handicaps, 21*, 72-80.

Kliewer, S. (1999). Seeking the functional. *Mental Retardation, 37*, 151-154.

McWilliam, R.A. (1996). A program of research on integrated vs. isolated treatment in early intervention. In R.A. McWilliam (Ed.), *Rethinking pull-out services in early intervention: A professional resource* (pp. 71-102). Baltimore: Paul H. Brookes.

Okagaki, L., Diamond, K.E., Kontos, S., & Hestenes, L. (1998). Correlates of young children's interactions with classmates with disabilities. *Early Childhood Research Quarterly, 13*, 67-86.

Peck, C.A., Carlson, P., & Helmstetter, E. (1992). Parent and teacher perceptions of outcomes for non-handicapped children enrolled in integrated early childhood programs: A statewide study. *Journal of Early Intervention, 16*, 53-63.

Ramsey, P.G. & Myers, L.C. (1990). Salience of race in young children's cognitive, affective, and behavioral responses to social environments. *Journal of Applied Developmental Psychology, 11*, 49-67.

Richardson, P. & Schwartz, I.S. (1998). Making friends in preschool: Friendship patterns of young children with disabilities. In L.H. Meyer, H.S. Park, M. Grenot-Scheyer, I.S. Schwartz, & B. Harry (Eds.), *Making friends: The influences of culture and development* (pp. 65-80). Baltimore: Paul H. Brookes.

Salisbury, C. & Palombaro, M. (1998). Friends and acquaintances: Evolving relationships in an inclusive elementary school. In L.H. Meyer, H.S. Park, M. Grenot-Scheyer, I.S. Schwartz, & B. Harry (Eds.), *Making friends: The influences of culture and development* (pp. 81-104). Baltimore: Paul H. Brookes.

Schnorr, R. (1990). "Peter? He comes and goes. . .": First graders' perspectives on a part-time mainstream student. *Journal of the Association for Persons with Severe Handicaps, 15*, 231-240.

Stoneman, Z. (1993). Attitudes toward young children with disabilities: Cognition, affect, and behavioral intent. In C. Peck, S. Odom, & D. Bricker (Eds.), *Integrating young children with disabilities in community programs: From research to implementation* (pp. 223-248). Baltimore: Paul H. Brookes.

Turnbull, A.P., Pereira, L., & Blue-Banning, M.J. (1999). Parents' facilitation of friendships between their children with a disability and friends without a disability. *Journal of the Association for Persons with Severe Handicaps, 24*, 85-99.

Turnbull, R. & Turnbull, A. P. (1991). Including all children. *Children Today, 20*(2), 3-5.

U.S. Census Bureau (1998). *Current population survey report: School enrollment – social and economic characteristics of students*. Washington, DC: U.S. Census Bureau.

Wolery, M., Holcombe, A., Brookfield, S., Huffman, K., Schroeder, C., Martin, C.G., Venn, M.L., Werts, M.G., & Fleming, L.A. (1993). The extent and nature of preschool mainstreaming: A survey of general early educators. *The Journal of Special Education, 27*, 222-234.

Passports for Learning in Inclusive Settings

Karla Hull, **Ed.D.**, Valdosta State University
Martha L. Venn, **Ph.D.**, Valdosta State University
Julia M. Lee, **Ph.D.**, Valdosta State University
Melissa Van Buren, **M.A.**, Valdosta State University

You can make the most out of a child's preschool experience by planning for his or her success in your program. In a sense, you are preparing a passport for the child's learning in your setting. You can think of a passport as a document that verifies who you are and provides entry or access into new activities and experiences. In the same way, passports for learning provide a way of thinking about the unique characteristics of an individual child in order to plan for his or her active participation in a variety of settings and activities.

Young children with disabilities enrolled in typical early childhood settings have enormous opportunities for increasing their developmental competence. In fact, inclusive preschool settings have been found to facilitate increased social competence and advanced play skills while providing more opportunities for children to practice newly acquired skills in functional settings (Demchak & Drinkwater, 1992; Diamond, Hestenes, & O'Connor, 1994). However, simply attending typical preschool programs is not enough. It takes a team of adults including the child's primary caregivers, preschool teachers, and possibly related service professionals (speech/language pathologists, occupational therapists, physical therapists) to ensure that a child with disabilities has access to and is supported in taking advantage of the preschool experiences that are available (Minzenberg, Laughlin, & Kaczmarek, 1999). How can you ensure that the children in your care are getting the most out of your early childhood environment?

"Can-Do" Thinking

You can begin to develop a child's passport by learning what the child **can do** and what he or she prefers to do in several activities or routines throughout the preschool day. We call this "can-do" thinking because it focuses on noticing a child's preferences and identifying the ways in which a child typically functions in a particular setting (Hull, Capone, Giangreco, Ross-Allen, 1996). This can-do model is based on research related to the role of children's preferences in learning and on intervention strategies that are embedded in everyday routines (Bricker, Pretti-Frontczak, McComas, 1998; Dyer, Dunlap, & Winterling, 1990; Koegel, Dyer, & Bell, 1987; Venn, Wolery, Fleming et al., 1993; Wolery, 1994).

There are many reasons for focusing on children's preferences including the fact that young children with disabilities are more engaged in activities they prefer, thus reducing inappropriate behaviors and increasing their learning (Dyer, Dunlap, & Winterling, 1990; Koegel, Dyer, & Bell, 1987). Understanding what a child can do during daily activities and routines provides the basis for embedding focused learning opportunities throughout the day through the use of activity-based interventions (Bricker, Pretti-Frontczak, & McComas, 1998), incidental, and milieu teaching (Hart & Risley, 1980; Kaiser, Yoder, & Keetz, 1992; Venn, Wolery, Werts, et al., 1993).

You can learn about children's functional competence through direct observation and by collaborating with the child's caregivers to determine ways in which the child typically acts and/or reacts to various activities and routines. You will want to know what children prefer and what they can do in a variety of activities and settings.

What Does Shelby Love to do?

Shelby is a four-year-old child with Down syndrome recently enrolled in an inclusive preschool program located in an elementary school building. She will be learning with a group of 21 other preschool children with and without disabilities. After observing Shelby as she played in the preschool classroom, Shelby's team (her mother, speech/language pathologist, preschool teacher, and special educator) met to talk about making the most out of Shelby's preschool experience. They began by looking at Shelby's preferences using the following questions to guide their discussion:

• What is Shelby interested in doing?
• If given a choice in this preschool setting, where would she spend most of her time?

• What are her preferences for materials and other children?
• Is there a particular time of day when she is more active?

These questions enabled the team to identify the kinds of activities that might attract Shelby's attention so that they could create a comfortable and engaging environment where new learning experiences could be built into Shelby's preferred activities.

What CAN Shelby DO?

The Can-Do Chart is one planning vehicle that you can use to assist in writing down exactly what you see a child doing during several key activities/routines in your classroom or childcare setting. Figure 1 provides an example of Shelby's Can-Do Chart.

Figure 1: Shelby's Can-Do Chart

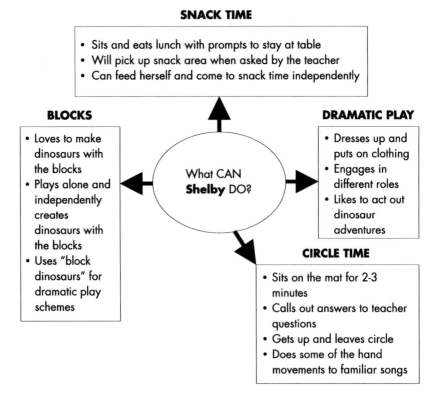

SNACK TIME
• Sits and eats lunch with prompts to stay at table
• Will pick up snack area when asked by the teacher
• Can feed herself and come to snack time independently

BLOCKS
• Loves to make dinosaurs with the blocks
• Plays alone and independently creates dinosaurs with the blocks
• Uses "block dinosaurs" for dramatic play schemes

What CAN Shelby DO?

DRAMATIC PLAY
• Dresses up and puts on clothing
• Engages in different roles
• Likes to act out dinosaur adventures

CIRCLE TIME
• Sits on the mat for 2-3 minutes
• Calls out answers to teacher questions
• Gets up and leaves circle
• Does some of the hand movements to familiar songs

If you look at Shelby's Can-Do Chart you will know what she typically does in various activities. This information was added to other information from Shelby's mother to develop a summary of her competencies. An inventory such as the one in Figure 2 can be filled out collaboratively between primary caregivers and preschool or early intervention professionals to assist in summarizing children's abilities and needs.

Figure 2: Shelby's Can-Do Inventory

I. Mobility
   A. What are the ways in which **Shelby** moves from place-to-place?

II. Communication
   A. I know that **Shelby** understands because she:
   B. **Shelby** tells me what she wants, likes, and doesn't like by:

III. Intellectual Growth
   A. **Shelby** lets me know what she is thinking by:
   B. **Shelby** learns new things easiest by:

IV. Self Care
   A. **Shelby** helps with dressing and bathing by:
   B. **Shelby** helps with eating and toileting by:

V. Socialization
   A. **Shelby** socializes and relates to other children by:
   B. **Shelby** socializes and relates to family members by:

VI. Play
   A. The ways in which **Shelby** plays with other children can be described by:
   B. The ways in which **Shelby** plays with objects/toys can be described by:
   C. The ways in which **Shelby** interacts with books can be described by:

Planning for Effective Inclusion Experiences

Planning is a crucial factor in the effectiveness of inclusive settings for young children with disabilities (Salisbury, Mangino, Petrigala, Rainforth, & Syryca, 1994; Santos, Lignugaris/Kraft, & Akers, 1999; Venn, 1997; Wolery, 1994). By examining your learning environment you can begin to identify the ways you can modify your typical routines and roles to more fully support all of the children in your care.

What CAN the Teacher DO?

Having gathered information about Shelby's abilities and preferences, her team began to think about the activities, routines, materials, and teacher's roles in Shelby's preschool classroom. They examined what Shelby would be expected to do throughout the day and where she would need support to experience the environment more fully. Shelby's team used the following questions to guide their analysis of her preschool classroom.

1. *What is the structure of the daily preschool activities and routines?* All routines and activities have a beginning, middle, and an end. If you carefully analyze each component of the activity/routine, you can identify or build in opportunities to address children's unique needs.

2. *What are the expectations for the children in activities/routines?* Often times you have spoken and unspoken expectations for children during a particular activity/routine. Your expectations may be based on viewing the children as a collective "we" or "group" instead of thinking about the strengths and needs of an individual child within the group. You will want to understand how each individual child responds to an activity/routine and ask yourself whether your expectations for children match their developmental needs and unique preferences.

3. *What kinds of roles do the teachers adopt throughout the day?* You wear many hats across the day, often changing hats on a moment-by-moment basis. During planning, take a look at your typical roles during a particular activity/routine. You may be able to identify what you do that supports children to be successful during the activity/routine, as well as clarify the new roles that you may need to assume to assist a particular child to be successful.

Figure 3, *Analyzing Daily Routines*, presents an example of the kinds of questions you might ask to guide your thinking as you analyze your activities or routines.

Figure 3: Analyzing Daily Routines

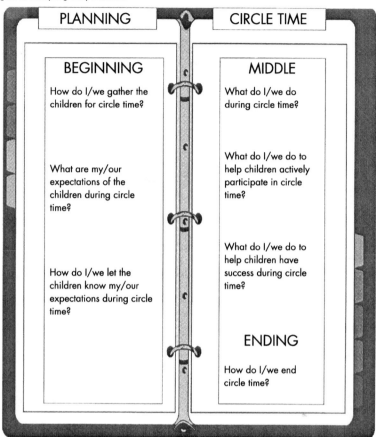

Identifying Daily Passport Objectives

Shelby has an Individualized Education Plan (IEP) with annual goals and objectives related to increasing the length of time she is engaged in activities and increasing the quality and quantity of her communication. Her team wanted to ensure that those goals and objectives were addressed throughout the day so that Shelby would be given multiple opportunities to learn and practice new skills. With the IEP document as a road map, Shelby's team used their knowledge of what Shelby could do and looked at the expectations and characteristics of her learning environment. In this way they were able to determine specific ways to support Shelby in getting the most out of her preschool experience. The following questions were used to determine the kinds of daily objectives that would enable Shelby to get more out of circle time and increase her knowledge and skills.

Given what **Shelby** currently does during circle time, do we want her to:

- **Do the same behavior:**
  - In more areas of the room?
  - With new partners?
  - For longer periods of time?
  - During new activities?
- **Learn a new behavior?**
- **Increase the complexity of the current behavior by:**
  - Adding new steps?
  - Increasing accuracy?

Shelby's team decided that they would like her to sit on the mat (a behavior she is already doing) for longer periods of time and be more actively engaged in the circle time activities. Since she is already doing some of the movements to familiar songs the team decided that they would like to see Shelby increase the complexity of that behavior by encouraging her to sing a few of the words to the songs. How will the teachers accomplish this? They can use all of the previously gathered information (Can-Do Chart and Can-Do Inventory) to create a plan for including Shelby.

Creating a Responsive Environment

The final step is to create a match between Shelby's abilities and needs and the classroom learning environment. Information collected for her learning passport provides the framework for the development of a responsive environment. The preschool environment includes the schedule of activities, the types of materials and toys used in various activities and routines, and the types of interactions among children as well as between children and teachers (Bailey & Wolery, 1992). An individual planning sheet, as presented in Figure 4, is helpful to identify possible changes in activity schedules, materials used, and teacher support necessary for Shelby to maximize her learning in this preschool program.

Figure 4: Individual Circle Time Planning

What do other children typically do during this activity/routine?	What does Shelby typically do during this activity/routine?	What are Shelby's Passport objectives?	What does the teacher do to support Shelby during this activity/routine?
• Most children sit on the mat for 20 minutes. • Most children raise their hand to respond to teacher questions. • Most children sing the words and do the hand movements to familiar songs.	• Shelby sits on the mat for 2-3 minutes. • Shelby calls out answers to teacher questions. • Shelby gets up and leaves circle. • Shelby does some of the hand movements to familiar songs.	• Shelby will sit on the mat for longer periods of time. • Shelby will be more involved in action songs by singing words as well as doing movements.	• I can sit next to Shelby and encourage her participation. • I will increase the physical movement activities during circle time and reduce sitting/listening time. • Shelby will be encouraged to choose her favorite song during circle time.

Taking information from *Shelby's Can-Do Chart* and *Shelby's Can-Do Inventory* based on the activities and routines in the classroom, the team targeted passport objectives for Shelby. In creating a responsive environment, you will want to determine if the schedule or length of the activities and routines needs to be modified to be more responsive to children's needs. As can be seen in Shelby's individual planning sheet, the teacher plans to sit next to her during circle time to help her stay on the mat for longer periods of time. Another possible action could be for the circle time to be reduced or split into two time periods, with Shelby's favorite activities occurring first. The circle time could then gradually be increased in length of time. The types of materials present in the environment could be changed by giving Shelby props to use while singing, which may increase her participation. Opportunities for interactions, including instructional interactions, should be planned and monitored for Shelby. These instructional interactions may consist of environmental changes (e.g., use of novel materials) or more direct teaching strategies. Finally, within a responsive environment, Shelby's passport will be continually updated to ensure effective communication, collaboration, and an environment that is responsive to her changing strengths and needs.

Note

Karla Hull can be reached by e-mail at khull@valdosta.edu

References

Bailey, D.B. & Wolery, M. (1992). Designing and arranging environments. In D. Bailey & M. Wolery (Eds.), *Teaching infants and preschoolers with disabilities* (2nd ed.) (pp. 198-228). New York: Macmillan Publishing Company.

Bricker, D., Pretti-Frontczak, K., & McComas, N. (1998). *An activity based approach to early intervention: Second edition.* Baltimore: Paul H. Brookes.

Demchak, M.A. & Drinkwater, S. (1992). Preschoolers with severe disabilities: The case against segregation. *Topics in Early Childhood Special Education, 11,* 70-83.

Diamond, K.E., Hestenes, L.L., & O'Connor, C.E. (1994). Integrating young children with disabilities in preschool: Problems and promise. *Young Children, 49,* 68-75.

Dyer, K., Dunlap, G., & Winterling, V. (1990). Effects of choice making on the serious problem behaviors of students with severe handicaps. *Journal of Applied Behavior Analysis, 23,* 515-524.

Hart, B. & Risley, T.R. (1980). In vivo language intervention: Unanticipated general effects. *Journal of Applied Behavior Analysis, 8,* 407-432.

Hull, K., Capone, A., Giangreco, M., & Ross-Allen, J. (1996). Through their eyes: Creating functional, child-sensitive, individualized education programs. In R.A. McWilliam (Ed.), *Rethinking pull-out services in early intervention: A professional resource* (pp. 103-119). Baltimore: Paul H. Brookes.

Kaiser, A., Yoder, P., & Keetz, A. (1992). Evaluating milieu teaching. In S.F. Warren & J. Reichle (Eds.), *Causes and effects in communication and language intervention: Volume 1* (pp. 9-47). Baltimore: Paul H. Brookes.

Koegel, R.L., Dyer, K., & Bell, L.K. (1987). The influence of child-preferred activities on autistic children's social behavior. *Journal of Applied Behavior Analysis, 20,* 243-252.

Minzenberg, B., Laughlin, J., & Kaczmarek, L., (1999). Early childhood special education in the developmentally appropriate classroom: A framework for conversation. *Young Exceptional Children, 2,* 10-17.

Salisbury, C.L., Mangino, M., Petrigala, M., Rainforth, B., & Syryca, S. (1994). Promoting the instructional inclusion of young children with disabilities in the primary grades. *Journal of Early Intervention, 18,* 311-322.

Santos, R.M., Lignugaris/Kraft, B., & Akers, J. (1999). Tips on planning center time activities for preschool classrooms. *Young Exceptional Children, 2,* 9-16.

Venn, M.L. (1997). *Exploring the long- and short-term planning practices of Head Start teachers with regards to children with and without disabilities.* Unpublished doctoral dissertation, University of Illinois at Urbana-Champaign, Champaign.

Venn, M.L., Wolery, M., Fleming, L., DeCesare, L., Morris, A., & Sigesmund, M.H. (1993). Effects of teaching preschool peers to use the mand-model procedure during snack activities. *American Journal of Speech-Language Pathology: A Journal of Clinical Practice,* 38-46.

Venn, M.L., Wolery, M., Werts, M.G., Morris, A., DeCesare, L., & Sigesmund, M.H. (1993). Using progressive time delay in arts/crafts activities to teach peer imitation to preschoolers with disabilities. *Early Childhood Research Quarterly, 8*(3), 277-295.

Wolery, M. (1994). Implementing instruction for young children with special needs in early childhood classrooms. In M. Wolery & J.S. Wilbers (Eds.), *Including children with special needs in early childhood programs* (pp. 97-118). NAEYC: Washington, DC.

Resources
Within Reason
Natural Environments and Inclusion

Here you'll find additional resources to support the successful inclusion of infants, toddlers, and young children in every day routines, activities, and places. Resources range in price. Many are within an individual's budget while others may be more suitable for acquisition by an agency or school.

Camille Catlett, M.A., University of North Carolina at Chapel Hill

Books

An Activity-Based Approach to Early Intervention (2nd ed.)

by D. Bricker, K. Pretti-Frontczak, & N. McComas

This extensively revised second edition shows how to use natural and relevant events to teach infants and young children of all abilities effectively and efficiently. An easy-to-use format details how and why activity-based intervention (ABI) can benefit any child through skillful applications in home and community settings. Baltimore: Paul Brookes.

Child Care+ Curriculum on Inclusion: Practical Strategies for Early Childhood Programs

Montana University Affiliated Rural Institute on Disabilities

The approach taken by this curriculum is unique: it suggests that by providing high quality care, young children of all abilities will grow and learn successfully. Through twelve chapters, information is offered that ranges from the history of inclusion to building partnerships with families and arranging the environment for learning. Activities, examples, and forms are provided throughout.

Montana University Affiliated Rural Institute on Disabilities
The University of Montana
634 Eddy Avenue
Missoula, MT 59812-6696
(406) 243-6355
Fax: (406) 243-4730
Web site: www.ccplus.org

Inclusive Schooling Practices: Pedagogical and Research Foundations: A Synthesis of the Literature That Informs Best Practices About Inclusive Schooling

G. McGregor, & R. T. Vogelsberg

Here's a great resource with a long, boring title. This publication provides a thoughtful synthesis of the literature on best practices about inclusive schooling. Methods, models, cases, and examples abound, and outcomes are elaborated by group (children with disabilities, children without disabilities, parents, teachers, etc.). Royalties from the sale of this publication are being donated to the Public Interest Law Center of Philadelphia in support of their ongoing efforts to assist families in obtaining inclusive services for their children. Baltimore: Paul Brookes.

Strategies for Preschool Intervention in Everyday Settings (SPIES): A Video-Assisted Program for Educators and Families

S. Rule, & B. Lancelot

Designed for use in everyday settings, these very thorough materials introduce strategies that can be used to help children learn and master new skills. Facilitator materials, participant materials, and companion videotapes also offer specific examples for working with infants and toddlers. While costly to purchase, the *SPIES* materials are available free of charge (http://www.cpd. usu.edu/SPIES/default.htm) to agencies, colleges and universities, and other organizations if they use them in teaching adults.

Connie Panter
Center for Persons with Disabilities
Utah State University
6800 Old Main Hill
Logan, UT 84322-6818
(435) 797-1993
FAX: (435) 797-3944
E-mail: connie@cpd2.usu.edu
Web site: http://www.cpd.usu.edu/SPIES/default.htm

Other Resources

ABCs of Inclusive Child Care

Dependent Care Management Group

This 14-minute videotape has many appealing features: culturally diverse parents, providers, and children illustrating the benefits of inclusion, closed captioning, and a perfect price—free and copyable. It's a well made, enjoyable to watch overview that's perfect for introducing the topic of inclusion of young children with disabilities in natural environments.

> Texas Planning Council on Developmental Disabilities
> 4900 N. Lamar Blvd
> Austin, TX 78751-2399
> (512) 424-4080; TTY: (512) 424-4099; (800) 262-0334;
> FAX: (512) 424-4097
> E-mail: txddc@rehab.state.tx.us
> Web site: http://www.rehab.state.tx.us/tpcdd/index.htm

Being a Kid: Services and Supports in Everyday Routines, Activities and Places

L. Edelman (Producer)

Here are six minutes of vignettes of a physical therapist working with a young child and his family at a neighborhood playground. Through reflective interviews, the video shows the therapist and the family working collaboratively to integrate functional therapy goals into daily routines and places.

> Western Media Products
> P.O. Box 591
> Denver, CO 80201
> (800) 232-8902
> FAX: (303) 455-5302
> Web site: http://www.media-products.com

Family-Guided Activity-Based Intervention for Infants and Toddlers

J. W. Cripe (Executive Producer), & J. Crabtree (Director)

Using this practical videotape, early childhood professionals will be able to teach parents and other caregivers how to use daily routines and activities to help young children with special needs gain vital skills in home and community settings. Among the topics covered are activity-based teaching methods that enhance children's development, accommodate families' daily schedules, address children's IFSP goals, and promote family interactions. Baltimore: Paul Brookes.

Same Time, Same Place

Purdue University, Continuing Education Administration

This videotape features children with disabilities in a variety of settings. Emphasis is placed on the roles and responsibilities of diverse partners (family, teachers, medical personnel, therapists) in supporting the inclusion process for children with severe disabilities in child care centers and family day care homes.

Self-directed Learning Programs
Purdue University
1586 Stuart Center, Room 116
West Lafayette, IN 47907
(800) 830-0269
Fax: (765) 496-2484

To Have a Friend

Portage Project

This video features six minutes of beautiful images of young friends of diverse cultures and abilities in a range of natural environments. It's a great icebreaker, discussion starter, or closing statement. Discussion questions and suggested activities are included.

Portage Project
CESA 5
626 East Slifer Street
Portage, WI 53901
(800) 862-3725 x268
Fax: (608) 742-2384
Web site: www.portageproject.org/brochure/mat_ls.htm

Yes, You Can Do It! Caring for Infants and Toddlers With Disabilities in Family Child Care

Children's Foundation

This 15-minute videotape offers very positive images and messages from parents and child care providers on the benefits of serving young children with disabilities. The accompanying manual, *Caring for Infants and Toddlers in Family Day Care: Annotated Resource Directory*, offers additional resources to support inclusion.

Children's Foundation Publications Department
725 15th Street, NW Suite 505
Washington, DC 20005-2109
(202) 347-3300
Fax: (202) 347-3382
Web site: www.childrensfoundation.net

Web Site Resources

Circle of Inclusion

A web site for early childhood service providers and families of young children that offers demonstrations (nine media-rich site visit options), information about effective practices of inclusive educational programs for children birth through age eight, as well as guidelines, forms, manuals, articles, and other materials.

Available online at http://www.circleofinclusion.org/

Early Childhood Research Institute on Inclusion (ECRII)

This five year national research project to study the inclusion of preschool children with disabilities in typical preschool, child care, and community settings has developed resources that include an annotated bibliography of research reports, position papers, books, special issues, and other resources.

Available online at http://www.fpg.unc.edu/~ecrii/

Family-Guided Approaches to Collaborative Early-Intervention Training and Services (FACETS)

Family stories, training modules, and instructional activities to build skills for supporting development in natural environments are among the resources provided.

Available online at http://www.parsons.lsi.ukans.edu/facets/

Inclusion: Yours, Mine, Ours

This site was developed by a group of teachers who believe in inclusion and want to offer support for others who are facing the daily challenges of creating successful inclusion experiences. Research information, real life success stories, and strategies for managing challenging behaviors are a few of the many areas addressed.

Available online at http://rushservices.com/Inclusion/

Keys to Inclusion

The National Early Childhood Technical Assistance System (NECTAS) web site was developed to build administrative supports for inclusion and natural environments. Features include examples of effective practices, fiscal resources, collaborative activities, research, laws, and policies.

Available online at http://www.nectas.unc.edu/inclusion/

Setting the Stage: Including Children With Disabilities in Head Start

If you're looking for detailed, practical information, activities, and handouts on inclusion, this resource may be just the ticket.

Available online at http://www.bmcc.org/Headstart/Setting/preface.htm

To order more copies of *Natural Environments and Inclusion*, contact:

> **Division for Early Childhood (DEC)**
> 27 Fort Missoula Road, Ste. 2
> Missoula, MT 59804
> (406) 543-0872
> FAX (406) 543-0887
> Email: dec@dec-sped.org
> www.dec-sped.org